Contents

1. Introduction   1

2. Understanding Your Mind   8

3. Thoughts and Feelings   27

4. Navigation Challenges   77

5. Building Strong Connections   121

6. Who Am I?   168

7. Overcoming Obstacles   186

8. Making Changes Last   211

9. Moving Forward   234

10. Navigating Tough Terrain   253

Appendix A   263

Appendix B   264

Appendix C   265

INTRODUCTION

Hello, remarkable teens!

Get ready to step into a world of self-discovery and personal empowerment with *Therapy Vibes: A Workbook for Teenagers*. This isn't just a workbook; it's your personal guide to mastering your emotions, making better choices, and thriving during your teenage years.

Unlocking the Power of Integration: Your Key to Emotional Well-Being

What sets this book apart is its innovative approach. It seamlessly integrates three powerful therapy approaches: CBT (Cognitive-Behavioral Therapy), DBT (Dialectical Behavior Therapy), and ACT (Acceptance and Commitment Therapy).

Now, you might be wondering, "What's the big deal about this integration?" Well, here's the scoop: these therapies are like individual pieces of a puzzle. CBT helps you understand your thoughts, DBT assists with managing emotions, and ACT guides you to live in alignment with your values. But when you put these pieces together, you create a complete picture of emotional well-being.

For Everyone, Whether You're a Pro or Newcomer

Whether you've never heard of these therapies before or you're already familiar with them, this workbook is for everyone. If you're learning these skills for the first time, that's fantastic. If you're honing your existing knowledge, you're in the right place. And if you're looking for a fresh angle on these approaches, you're in for a treat.

Let's break it down with a relatable example:

Imagine you're in this situation—an argument with a close friend.

- **CBT**: Cognitive-Behavioral Therapy helps you recognize negative thought patterns that can escalate conflicts. For instance, you might catch yourself thinking, "My friend never listens to me; they don't care." CBT encourages you to challenge this thought by looking for evidence to the contrary. Maybe you recall instances where your friend has been attentive.

- **ACT**: Acceptance and Commitment Therapy guide you in accepting difficult emotions that arise during the argument. Instead of suppressing your frustration, you acknowledge it without judgment. ACT reminds you that it's okay to feel upset while encouraging you to stay committed to your values, which might include maintaining healthy relationships.

- **DBT**: Dialectical Behavior Therapy equips you with emotion regulation skills to manage intense feelings. When the argument triggers strong emotions, DBT techniques, like mindfulness exercises, can help you stay grounded in the present moment, preventing impulsive reactions.

In this scenario, these three approaches blend seamlessly, helping you navigate the argument constructively. This is just a taste of how this workbook's integration empowers you to address real-life situations effectively. And remember, this workbook is not an exhaustive guide; it focuses on the most valuable concepts and skills proven to work.

So, as you embark on this journey, know that you're equipped with a holistic toolkit that can adapt to various situations. Your growth is a unique adventure, and we're here to guide you every step of the way.

The Holistic Advantage

Now, it's important to note that this workbook isn't an exhaustive encyclopedia of these therapies. It doesn't cover every single concept or technique. Instead, it's designed to focus on the most high-yield, effective skills—the ones that will make the most significant impact on your emotional well-being.

In a nutshell, the holistic integration of CBT, DBT, and ACT in this workbook is your key to unlocking a more balanced, fulfilled, and confident version of yourself. It's about taking the best concepts and skills from each approach to create a practical and effective guide for your emotional well-being journey.

Why Your Emotional Well-being Matters

This workbook is all about one thing—your emotional well-being. It's the cornerstone of everything we'll explore, and here's why it matters:

1. **Quality of Life:** Your emotional well-being significantly impacts your overall quality of life. It's about feeling content, satisfied, and genuinely happy with the life you're living. When you're emotionally well, you wake up each day with a sense of joy and purpose, excited to face what lies ahead.

   - *Imagine Sam and Alex: Sam, with strong emotional well-being, manages emotions effectively, seeks out activities they enjoy, and maintains a positive outlook on life. This leads to a greater sense of contentment. In contrast, Alex struggles with emotional well-being, often feeling overwhelmed by stress and negative emotions. Over time, Alex's overall quality of life suffers due to chronic stress and unhappiness.*

2. **Healthy Relationships:** Emotional well-being is the glue that holds healthy relationships together. It's about understanding your emotions and those of the people around you. When you're emotionally well, you can communicate openly, empathize, and connect with others on a deeper level.

   - *Consider a Disagreement: Imagine you and a friend have a disagreement. If you both have strong emotional well-being, you're more likely to communicate openly, understand each other's perspectives, and resolve the conflict in a way that strengthens your friendship. Conversely, if one or both of you struggle with emotional well-being, the disagreement may escalate, leading to strained relations and hurt feelings.*

3. **Resilience:** Emotional well-being is your shield against life's challenges. It's your ability to bounce back from setbacks, adapt to changes, and maintain your equilibrium even in turbulent times. It's not just about surviving; it's about thriving in the face of adversity.

   - *Meet Emily and Jake: Picture a student, Emily, who faces a challenging academic semester with numerous exams and projects. Emily possesses strong emotional well-being; she practices stress-management techniques, seeks support when needed, and maintains a positive mindset. As a result, she not only performs well but also bounces back from setbacks, demonstrating resilience. In contrast, another student, Jake, neglects his emotional well-being, leading to stress, anxiety, and a decrease in academic performance.*

4. **Decision-Making:** Emotional well-being is at the core of effective decision-making. It's about understanding your emotions, values, and desires and using that knowledge to make choices that align with your long-term goals and aspirations.

   - *Meet Lily and Max: Picture a teenager, Lily, who is offered the opportunity to join a new extracurricular activity. She's in tune with her emotions, understands her interests and values, and recognizes that the activity aligns with her passion for helping others. Lily's decision to join the activity is driven by her emotional well-being and leads to a fulfilling experience. In contrast, her friend Max makes decisions without considering his emotions or values and often ends up feeling unsatisfied with his choices.*

The Dangers of Neglecting Emotional Well-being

Now, let's talk about the flip side—the dangers of neglecting your emotional well-being:

1. **Stress and Burnout:** Neglecting your emotional well-being can lead to chronic stress and eventual burnout. It's like carrying a heavy backpack filled with worries and anxieties that never seem to lighten.

   ○ *Imagine Sarah's Overload: Consider a college student, Sarah, who constantly ignores her emotional well-being by overloading herself with coursework and extracurricular activities. Over time, her stress levels soar, and she begins to experience burnout. This not only impacts her academic performance but also takes a toll on her physical health, leading to chronic headaches and exhaustion.*

2. **Strained Relationships:** Neglecting emotional well-being can strain your relationships with others. It's like speaking a different emotional language, leading to misunderstandings and conflicts.

   ○ *Sibling Struggles: Picture two siblings, Mia and Ethan, who struggle to communicate effectively due to their neglected emotional well-being. They frequently misinterpret each other's actions and words, leading to arguments and a strained sibling relationship. Their failure to understand and manage their emotions contributes to ongoing conflicts.*

3. **Unfulfillment:** Neglecting your emotional well-being may lead to a sense of unfulfillment and a lack of purpose. It's like searching for a missing piece of a puzzle that completes the picture of your life.

   ○ *Jamie's Quest for Fulfillment: Consider a person named Jamie, who goes through life without exploring their emotional landscape and passions. Jamie never takes the time to reflect on their true interests and values. As a result, they often feel unfulfilled and struggle to find a sense of purpose, leaving them with a nagging sense of emptiness.*

These examples illustrate the significant impact that emotional well-being can have on various aspects of life, as well as the potential consequences of neglecting it. By prioritizing emotional well-being, individuals can enhance their overall quality of life, relationships, resilience, decision-making, and personal growth.

Practical Tools for Real-Life Adventures

1. **Stress Management:** Life can throw curveballs your way, and stress is like the dragon you must conquer. For example, imagine you have a big test coming up, and you notice you're thinking, "I'm going to fail." You can use CBT to challenge this thought by considering evidence to the contrary, like previous successes, which can reduce stress. ACT principles will guide you in accepting stress as a natural part of life and focusing on actions aligned with your values. DBT skills may be integrated to help regulate intense emotions during stressful moments.

2. **Emotion Regulation:** Emotions can be like wild horses, but you'll learn how to be the master of your emotional realm. For instance, picture a moment when you feel overwhelmed with anger. DBT skills can help you "observe" and "describe" your anger without judgment, making it easier to manage and respond effectively. Additionally, CBT techniques may be incorporated to challenge and reframe unhelpful beliefs that contribute to emotional distress. ACT principles can guide you in accepting and allowing your emotions to be, even when they're challenging.

3. **Mindful Decision-Making:** Life is a series of choices, and you'll become a mindful decision-maker. Let's say you're deciding whether to stand up against a friend who's treating others unfairly. Using ACT, you can clarify your values and commit to a decision that aligns with your values, even if it's challenging. CBT will equip you with cognitive tools to evaluate the pros and cons of different decisions, helping you make choices that align with your values. DBT skills may come into play to regulate emotions when making significant decisions.

4. **Effective Communication:** Relationships are the heart of human experience, and effective communication is the key to nurturing them. Consider a situation where you feel anxious about speaking up in class. CBT can help you recognize and challenge "catastrophizing" thoughts, allowing you to communicate more confidently. ACT principles will encourage you to communicate authentically, aligning your actions with your values in your interactions with others. DBT's interpersonal effectiveness skills may be applied to navigate conflicts and improve communication in relationships.

5. **Goal Setting and Commitment:** Dream big, set goals, and turn your aspirations into reality. Let's say you have a goal to improve your physical fitness. ACT can help you set that goal based on your values, such as health and well-being, and commit to it, even when facing challenges like sore muscles or busy schedules. CBT will help you identify and challenge any self-limiting beliefs that might stand in the way of setting and achieving your goals. DBT skills may assist you in managing emotional challenges that arise during your goal pursuit.

6. **Mindful Living:** Embrace the present moment and live in harmony with your values. Imagine enjoying a

meal mindfully, savoring each bite without distractions. DBT mindfulness skills can help you "one-mind-fully" engage in activities, enhancing your experience. ACT principles will guide you in aligning your actions with your values, encouraging mindful living and a greater sense of purpose in daily life. CBT techniques can aid in identifying and challenging any cognitive patterns that interfere with mindful living.

Remember that these examples illustrate how these tools can be applied, and the combinations are infinite. One of the remarkable aspects of this holistic workbook is that the skills you'll acquire from CBT (Cognitive-Behavioral Therapy), ACT (Acceptance and Commitment Therapy), and DBT (Dialectical Behavior Therapy) are like versatile tools in your emotional toolbox. These tools aren't rigidly separated; instead, they often overlap and complement each other.

Imagine it like this: just as a Swiss Army knife has various functions neatly integrated into a single tool, your emotional well-being toolkit combines different therapeutic approaches, allowing you to tailor your response to different situations.

Your Journey Begins Now: Embrace the Power of Practice

Are you pumped up and ready to dive into this incredible journey of self-discovery? Fantastic! You're in for a treat. Just like everyone can dance in front of their own mirror, but when it comes to the big dance competition, practice becomes the secret sauce for success.

Think of it this way: you might understand the moves and grooves when you dance alone, but to shine on the competition stage, you've got to put in those practice hours. It's like the gamers who play casually versus those who become esports champions—it's all about the grind, the practice, and the dedication.

And guess what? This workbook is here to supercharge your practice sessions. It's filled with awesome worksheets that will make practicing these skills feel like leveling up in your favorite game. Because, as you'll soon discover, understanding these skills is just the first step—practice is where the real magic happens. So, grab your workbook, find a comfy spot, and get ready to conquer life's challenges like a pro!

Alongside these valuable worksheets, make sure to write down the content from each worksheet in your journal as you work through them. This way, you'll have all your thoughts and progress in one place. Just like dancers keep track of their routines or gamers note their strategies, your journal can be your go-to buddy during this journey. It's where you can jot down what you learn, those lightbulb moments, and the practice you put into these skills. So, be sure to jot down the worksheet stuff in your journal to make your self-improvement adventure even more epic!

How We Roll

Now, let's talk about how this book is gonna roll. Picture it like starting a new game. At the beginning, you're in the tutorial level, right? That's where we're at now. The first few chapters are gonna be longer, packed with all the juicy details and strategies you need to get started on your quest for self-discovery.

Think of it like building your character's skills – you gotta spend some time in the training grounds to become a true warrior. But as you progress through the game, things start to get easier. You'll notice the chapters getting shorter because you've already got the basics down. It's like skipping through those tutorial levels 'cause you already know how to swing your sword or cast spells.

So, don't be surprised if the chapters start to feel a bit shorter as we go along. It just means you're leveling up and becoming a master of this game called life. Get ready to crush those challenges and unlock your full potential!

2

UNDERSTANDING YOUR MIND

Introduction

Hey there, and welcome to your journey of self-discovery and growth! In this workbook, we're going to explore some awesome stuff that'll help you understand yourself better and navigate life like a pro.

First off, we'll briefly cover the basics of Cognitive-Behavioral Therapy (CBT), Acceptance and Commitment Therapy (ACT), and Dialectical Behavior Therapy (DBT). These are like your superpowers for dealing with all sorts of challenges and emotions.

Next, we'll take a peek into the teenage brain and how it works. Understanding how your brain ticks can help you make sense of your thoughts and feelings, which is pretty cool, right?

We'll also chat about mindfulness – it's like your secret weapon for staying calm and focused in a busy world. Mindfulness is a big deal in these therapies, so we'll make sure you're up to speed on it.

And then, we'll dive into self-assessment. This is where the real magic happens. It's like looking in a mirror and really seeing yourself for the first time. By checking in with yourself, you'll get a clearer picture of who you are and what you want out of life.

So, get ready to embark on this journey with us. The chapters ahead are filled with tips, tricks, and exercises to help you become the best version of yourself. Let's dive in and discover all the awesome things that make you, you!

Section 1: Introduction to CBT, ACT, and DBT

In this section, we'll dive into the foundational concepts of Cognitive-Behavioral Therapy (CBT), Acceptance and Commitment Therapy (ACT), and Dialectical Behavior Therapy (DBT). These therapeutic approaches may sound complex, but don't worry; we'll break them down into digestible bits

What Are CBT, ACT, and DBT?

Imagine you have a toolbox filled with different tools for various tasks. CBT, ACT, and DBT are like three powerful tools in your emotional toolbox, each designed for specific purposes. Let's explore what each of them does:

- **CBT (Cognitive-Behavioral Therapy):** CBT focuses on understanding and changing unhelpful thought patterns and behaviors. It helps you identify negative or irrational thoughts, challenge them, and replace them with more realistic and positive thoughts. Think of CBT as your "Thought Reframing Tool."

- **ACT (Acceptance and Commitment Therapy):** ACT centers around accepting your thoughts and feelings without judgment while committing to actions aligned with your values. It helps you move forward even when faced with challenging emotions. ACT is like your "Values and Commitment Tool."

- **DBT (Dialectical Behavior Therapy):** DBT teaches emotional regulation, distress tolerance, and mindfulness. It equips you with the skills to manage intense emotions, cope with crises, and stay grounded in the present moment. DBT acts as your "Emotional Mastery Tool."

Your Emotional Toolbox

Just as a mechanic relies on their tools to fix cars or a chef uses knives to prepare delicious meals, you can use these therapies as tools to enhance your emotional life. Each tool has its unique purpose, and throughout this workbook, you'll discover how to use them effectively in different situations.

In the subsequent chapters, we'll take a deeper dive into each of these therapies. You'll get to know them intimately, like the back of your hand. Together, we'll explore their core principles, techniques, and how to apply them in real-life situations. These chapters will be your guide to becoming proficient in using these valuable tools from your emotional toolbox.

Section 2: The Teenage Brain: Neuroscience of Teenage Development

In this section, we'll take a journey deep into the intricate world of neuroscience to understand what's happening inside your head during these transformative years. You'll discover why your brain is like a dynamic, ever-changing masterpiece and how this knowledge can empower you on your path to emotional well-being.

The Teenage Brain Unveiled

Your brain is an extraordinary organ that undergoes profound changes from childhood through adolescence and into adulthood. During your teenage years, it's like a bustling construction site, constantly building, remodeling, and fine-tuning its structures and connections. These changes are guided by a special team of architects known as hormones and fueled by experiences and emotions.

Why Understanding Your Brain Matters

Now, you might wonder, "Why should I care about what's happening inside my brain?" Well, here's the scoop: understanding your brain is like having a user manual for life. It helps you make sense of your thoughts, emotions, and behaviors. It's the key to unlocking your potential and making informed choices.

The Pre-Frontal Cortex: Your Brain's CEO

One of the critical areas we'll explore is the pre-frontal cortex (PFC), often referred to as the brain's CEO. This region is responsible for high-level thinking, decision-making, and controlling impulsive behaviors. Picture it as the control center of your brain, overseeing everything from planning your day to managing your emotions during a heated argument.

But here's the twist: while your PFC is undergoing significant development during your teenage years, it's not fully wired yet. That means it's like a work-in-progress, making decisions and solving problems with some bumps along the way. It's like driving a car that's still being assembled—functional, but not entirely fine-tuned.

By learning skills from therapies like CBT, ACT, and DBT, you're essentially providing your brain with the tools it needs to enhance the wiring of your PFC. You can become better at decision-making, emotional regulation, and planning for the future. It's like giving your brain an upgrade to be a more efficient CEO.

The Emotional Roller Coaster

You've probably noticed that your emotions can be like a roller coaster ride during adolescence. One moment, you're riding high on happiness, and the next, you're plummeting into a pit of despair. Blame it on your brain's limbic system, which plays a central role in emotions.

The limbic system, responsible for processing emotions, is like the heart of your emotional experiences. During adolescence, it's supercharged and highly sensitive, reacting strongly to events and situations. That's why you might feel emotions more intensely than you did as a child.

Skills from these therapies can help you learn to navigate this emotional roller coaster more effectively. They provide you with tools to understand your emotions, accept them without judgment, and respond to them in healthier ways. By doing so, you're essentially rewiring your brain to have more balanced emotional responses.

The Teen Brain's Superpower: Plasticity

Now, here's the exciting part: your teenage brain possesses an incredible superpower known as plasticity. No, it doesn't mean your brain is made of plastic, but rather that it's incredibly adaptable. Think of it as a superhero that can reshape itself based on your experiences and actions.

This plasticity is what makes adolescence a crucial period for growth and learning. It allows you to acquire new skills, adapt to different environments, and recover from setbacks. Your brain is like a sponge, soaking up knowledge and experiences to shape your future self.

The Impact on Emotional Well-Being

Understanding your developing brain is crucial for your emotional well-being. It explains why you might sometimes struggle with managing your emotions, making decisions, or handling stress. It's not because you're "broken" or "inconsistent," but because your brain is still a masterpiece in progress.

Art Activity: Mapping Your Teenage Brain

Let's get creative and dive into an art project that will help you explore the various aspects of your life that shape your teenage brain. In this activity, you'll create a brain map that reflects different parts of your life and how they impact your development.

Materials Needed:

- Large sheet of paper or poster board

- Markers, colored pencils, or crayons

- Scissors

- Old magazines or printed images

- Glue or tape

Instructions:

1. Begin by drawing the outline of a brain on the large sheet of paper or poster board. Make it as big as you'd like, leaving enough space for details.

2. Divide your brain into different sections or lobes, just like the brain's anatomy. You can label these sections based on the areas of your life you want to explore. For example, you might have sections like "School," "Family," "Friends," "Hobbies," "Goals," and "Challenges."

3. Now, it's time to fill in each section. For "School," you can draw or collage images related to your classes, teachers, and favorite subjects. In the "Family" section, include images or words that represent your family members and the role they play in your life. Continue this process for each section.

4. You can use words, drawings, or images from magazines to represent each aspect. If you enjoy writing, jot down a few sentences or thoughts about each section.

5. Pay attention to the size of each section. Make the sections larger or smaller depending on how important they are in your life. For example, if your friends play a significant role, their section might be bigger.

6. As you work on your brain map, reflect on how each part influences your teenage experience. What emotions, memories, or challenges are associated with them? How do they contribute to your growth and development?

7. Once you've completed your brain map, take a step back and admire your creation. It's a visual representation of the complex and multifaceted nature of your teenage brain.

8. If you're comfortable, share your brain map with friends, family, or a trusted adult. Discuss what you've learned about yourself and how these different aspects of your life interact.

Song Recommendation: "Colors" by Beck

⌐ Maybe put in bold?.

Section 3: Mindfulness (DBT): Mindfulness Exercises and Their Benefits for Teenagers

Welcome to the world of mindfulness—a powerful practice that can help you navigate the ups and downs of your teenage years with grace and resilience. In this section, we'll explore why mindfulness is such an essential tool on your journey of self-discovery and personal growth.

Why Mindfulness Matters

Mindfulness isn't just a trendy buzzword; it's a cornerstone of several therapeutic approaches, including Dialectical Behavior Therapy (DBT), Cognitive-Behavioral Therapy (CBT), and even Acceptance and Commitment Therapy (ACT). By introducing mindfulness here, we're setting the stage for the skills and techniques you'll learn throughout this workbook.

But what exactly is mindfulness, and why is it so important? At its core, mindfulness is about being fully present in the moment, without judgment. It's the practice of paying attention to your thoughts, feelings, and sensations as they arise, accepting them as they are, and letting them go. This might sound simple, but its impact is profound.

Mindfulness and Your Teenage Brain

Remember when we explored the neuroscience of teenage development? Well, here's where it all comes together. Your teenage brain is like a work in progress, with various parts developing at different rates. One area that's still under construction is the prefrontal cortex, responsible for decision-making, impulse control, and emotional regulation. That's why you might sometimes feel like your emotions are on a rollercoaster ride.

Mindfulness steps in as your brain's trusty sidekick. It helps you sharpen your focus, improve emotional regulation, and reduce impulsivity—all crucial skills as your brain matures. By practicing mindfulness, you're essentially rewiring your brain in more helpful ways. This rewiring process, known as neuroplasticity, allows you to build healthier habits and responses to life's challenges.

The Benefits of Mindfulness for Teenagers

So, what's in it for you? Why should you bother with mindfulness? Here are some of the fantastic benefits you can expect:

1. **Reduced Stress:** Teenage life can be stressful, with exams, social pressures, and personal expectations. Mindfulness can be your secret weapon against stress, helping you stay calm and composed even in

challenging situations.

2. **Improved Focus:** With so many distractions around, it's easy to lose focus. Mindfulness enhances your ability to concentrate, whether you're studying, engaging in a hobby, or simply enjoying the moment.

3. **Better Emotional Regulation:** Remember those intense emotions we discussed earlier? Mindfulness equips you with the skills to manage them effectively. Instead of reacting impulsively, you'll learn to respond thoughtfully and calmly.

4. **Enhanced Self-Awareness:** Mindfulness encourages self-reflection and self-awareness. You'll gain a deeper understanding of your thoughts, feelings, and behaviors, which can be incredibly empowering.

5. **Greater Resilience:** Life is full of ups and downs, and mindfulness helps you bounce back from setbacks. It teaches you to accept difficulties without judgment and to move forward with a positive mindset.

6. **Improved Relationships:** Mindfulness isn't just about your relationship with yourself; it also influences how you relate to others. By being present and attentive, you can strengthen your connections with friends and family.

Mindfulness in Various Therapies

Mindfulness isn't limited to just one type of therapy; it's a versatile tool that can enhance several therapeutic approaches. Here's how mindfulness can be used in different therapy scenarios:

- **Dialectical Behavior Therapy (DBT):** As you'll discover throughout this workbook, DBT heavily incorporates mindfulness practices. It's used to help individuals regulate emotions, tolerate distress, and improve interpersonal effectiveness.

- **Cognitive-Behavioral Therapy (CBT):** In CBT, mindfulness can be applied to challenge and reframe unhelpful thoughts and behaviors. It helps individuals gain awareness of their automatic thought patterns.

- **Acceptance and Commitment Therapy (ACT):** ACT encourages mindfulness to help individuals accept their thoughts and feelings without judgment. It's used to align actions with personal values and commit to meaningful goals.

So, get ready to embark on your mindfulness journey. Throughout this workbook, you'll find mindfulness exercises and practices designed to enhance your emotional well-being and equip you with valuable tools for life's adventures. Remember, mindfulness isn't just a practice; it's a way of life—a way that can lead to greater self-awareness, resilience, and a more fulfilling teenage experience.

Mindfulness Worksheet

How to Practice Mindfulness

Here's a detailed step-by-step guide on how to practice mindfulness. You can switch it up by finding a partner to read the guide:

1. **Find a Quiet Space:** To begin, choose a quiet and comfortable space where you won't be disturbed. It could be your bedroom, a park, or any place where you feel relaxed.

2. **Assume a Comfortable Posture:** Sit or lie down in a comfortable position. You can sit on a chair, cushion, or the floor with your back straight but not rigid. Rest your hands on your lap or knees.

3. **Focus on Your Breath:** Close your eyes if it feels comfortable for you. Begin by taking a few natural breaths, paying attention to the sensation of your breath entering and leaving your body.

4. **Deep Breathing:** Inhale slowly through your nose for a count of four seconds. Feel your chest and abdomen rise as you fill your lungs with air. Hold your breath for another four seconds.

5. **Exhale Slowly:** Exhale gently and completely through your mouth for a count of four seconds. Feel the tension leaving your body as you breathe out.

6. **Repeat:** Continue this mindful breathing pattern for a few minutes. As you breathe, focus your attention solely on the sensation of your breath—how it feels, the rhythm, and the movement of your chest and abdomen.

7. **Observe Your Thoughts:** During this practice, you may notice thoughts entering your mind. This is entirely normal. Instead of trying to push them away, acknowledge their presence without judgment. Imagine your thoughts as clouds passing by in the sky, and gently bring your focus back to your breath.

8. **Be Present:** As you continue mindful breathing, try to become fully present in the moment. Feel the connection between your body and the earth, the sensation of the air on your skin, and the sounds around you.

9. **Gradual Return:** After a few minutes, gradually return to your normal breathing pattern. Open your eyes if they were closed.

10. **Reflect:** Take a moment to reflect on how you feel after this mindfulness exercise. Do you notice any changes in your emotional state or physical sensations? Remember that mindfulness is a skill that becomes

more effective with practice, so be patient with yourself.

Set aside five minutes each day to practice mindful breathing. This exercise can be particularly helpful when you're feeling overwhelmed or anxious, as it provides a simple yet effective way to ground yourself in the present moment. Over time, you can extend the duration of your mindfulness practice as you become more comfortable with the technique.

Remember, mindfulness is a skill that can be developed over time with practice. As you continue through this workbook, you'll discover more mindfulness exercises and strategies to help you on your journey toward emotional well-being.

Song Recommendation: "Breathe" by Télépopmusik.

Section 4: Self-Assessment Activities

As we embark on this journey of self-discovery and personal growth, it's essential to have a clear understanding of where you currently stand. These self-assessment activities are designed to help you gain insights into your thoughts, emotions, values, and goals.

Self-Assessment Activity 1: Exploring Your Emotions

Understanding and managing your emotions is a crucial skill on your journey to improved emotional well-being. This questionnaire will help you explore and identify your emotions more clearly. Remember, it's normal to experience a wide range of emotions, and each one serves a purpose.

Instructions:

1. For each emotion listed below, rate how frequently you experience it on a scale from 1 to 5, with 1 being "Rarely" and 5 being "Frequently."

2. After rating each emotion, take a moment to reflect on situations or triggers that lead to that emotion.

Emotions:

1. Happiness – _____

2. Sadness – _____

3. Anger – _____

4. Fear – _____

5. Excitement – _____

6. Calmness – _____

7. Frustration – _____

8. Gratitude – _____

9. Anxiety – _____

10. Confusion – _____

Reflection:

Are there any patterns or common triggers you've noticed?

How comfortable do you feel when experiencing these emotions?

Are there any emotions you would like to better understand or manage?

Self-Assessment Activity 2: Understanding Your Values

This reflection exercise will help you gain clarity on what truly matters to you. Identifying your values is an essential step in making decisions that align with your authentic self.

Instructions:

1. Below, you'll find a list of common values. Circle the ones that resonate with you the most. Don't overthink it; go with your initial instinct.

2. After selecting your top values, take a moment to write a brief explanation of why each one is important to you.

List of Values:

I feel like the list needs :

- Family
- Friendship
- Adventure
- Creativity
- Honesty
- Independence
- Kindness
- Learning
- Nature
- Peace
- Health
- Love
- Equality
- Courage

Reflection:

Are there values you chose that surprise you? Why?

How do your values influence the decisions you make?

Are there any values you would like to prioritize more in your life?

Understanding your values will help you set meaningful goals and lead a life that aligns with your deepest desires and aspirations. It's a journey toward greater self-awareness and authenticity.

Self-Assessment Activity 3: Recognizing Negative Thoughts

Before we dive into challenging negative thoughts, it's important to become aware of them. This simple activity will help you recognize when negative thoughts creep into your mind.

Instructions:

1. Take a few moments to sit quietly, close your eyes if you'd like, and focus on your breathing.

2. Pay attention to your thoughts. What is your mind saying right now?

3. Jot down any negative thoughts that you notice. These could be self-critical, worrisome, or pessimistic thoughts.

Example Thoughts:

- "I'm not good at this."

- "Nobody likes me."

- "I'll never be able to do it."

Remember, everyone has negative thoughts from time to time. This activity is about becoming aware of them. In the following chapters, we'll explore strategies to challenge and reframe these thoughts to help you feel more positive and confident.

Self-Assessment Activity 4: Identifying Stressors

Stress is a common part of life, and understanding what causes your stress is the first step in managing it effectively. This questionnaire will help you identify specific stressors in your life.

Instructions:

1. Review the list of common stressors below.

2. Rate each stressor on a scale from 1 to 5, with 1 being "Not Stressful" and 5 being "Very Stressful."

3. Be honest with yourself, and consider how much each stressor currently affects you.

bigger space

- Schoolwork or exams: _____/5

- Family conflicts: _____/5

- Friendship or relationship issues: _____/5

- Peer pressure: _____/5

- Body image concerns: _____/5

- Personal health issues: _____/5

- Extracurricular activities: _____/5

- Future plans or career choices: _____/5

- Financial concerns: _____/5

- Other (Specify): _____/5

Once you've rated these stressors, you'll have a clearer picture of which areas in your life may need more attention when it comes to stress management. In later chapters, we'll explore techniques to help you cope with and reduce stress effectively.

Self-Assessment Activity 5: Setting Personal Goals

Setting goals can help you make positive changes in different areas of your life. This worksheet will help you get started on setting your personal goals.

Instructions:

1. Think about areas in your life where you'd like to make improvements or changes.

2. Write down a goal for each area. Make it simple and clear.

3. Use the examples below to help you.

Examples:

- Area: School

  ○ Goal: Improve my math grade from a C to a B by the end of this semester.

- Area: Personal Growth

  ○ Goal: Practice mindfulness for at least 10 minutes every day to reduce stress and improve focus.

- Area: Relationships

  ○ Goal: Strengthen my communication skills by having an open and honest conversation with a friend about an issue we've been avoiding.

Your Personal Goals:

Area 1: _____

Goal:

Area 2: _____

Goal:

Area 3: _____

Goal:

Remember, setting goals is a way to focus on what you want to achieve. Your goals can be big or small, but they should be things that matter to you. Start with a few, and as you go through this workbook, you can add more or adjust them as needed.

What to Expect Next

Congratulations! You've taken the first step in exploring your thoughts, emotions, and personal goals. The self-assessment activities you've completed are essential building blocks for your journey ahead.

In the upcoming chapters of this workbook, we will delve deeper into the principles of Cognitive-Behavioral Therapy (CBT), Acceptance and Commitment Therapy (ACT), and Dialectical Behavior Therapy (DBT). You'll learn specific strategies and techniques to help you navigate challenges, understand your emotions, build healthier relationships, and much more.

As you continue your exploration, keep in mind the areas you've identified through these self-assessment activities. The insights gained here will serve as a compass, guiding you toward the chapters and exercises most relevant to your personal growth. Each chapter is designed to help you develop the skills and knowledge needed to address the specific areas you've highlighted.

Remember, change and growth take time. Be patient with yourself as you embark on this journey of self-discovery and healing. You have the tools to make meaningful progress in the areas that matter most to you. Your commitment to this process is a significant step toward a happier and healthier you.

Stay curious, stay open, and keep moving forward. The next chapters will empower you with even more valuable insights and strategies to enhance your emotional well-being and reach your personal goals.

3

THOUGHTS AND FEELINGS

Introduction

Hey there, awesome readers! Welcome to Chapter 3 of our journey to understanding your mind and supercharging your emotional skills. In this chapter, we're diving deep into the fascinating world of thoughts and feelings, and let me tell you, this stuff can be a total game-changer!

Defining Thoughts and Feelings

First things first, what are thoughts and feelings?

- **Thoughts:** These are the words and sentences that pop into your mind. They're like the little thinkers in your brain, always chattering away. Thoughts can be positive, negative, or just random observations about the world around you.

- **Feelings:** These are the emotions that you experience. They can be joy, sadness, anger, fear, excitement, and many more. Feelings are like colorful clouds floating through your emotional sky.

Now, you might be wondering, "Why do we need to explore these things?" Well, here's the deal: thoughts and feelings are like two best friends who love hanging out together. They influence each other more than you'd imagine, and understanding this dynamic duo can transform your life.

Setting the Stage

Imagine you're standing in front of a giant domino setup. Each domino represents a thought, and the last domino represents your feelings. When you flick that first domino (a thought), it sets off a chain reaction, and all the dominoes (feelings) start falling one after the other.

For example, if you think, "I'm going to do great on this test," the positive thought can trigger feelings of confidence, happiness, and excitement. But if you think, "I'll never understand this math stuff," it can set off a chain of feelings like frustration, anxiety, and self-doubt.

So, how can understanding this be a game-changer? Well, imagine if you knew how to set up those dominoes (thoughts) in a way that led to positive feelings more often. You'd feel more confident, less stressed, and better equipped to tackle life's challenges.

How It's a Game-Changer

In real life, this understanding works wonders too. Let's say you have a big presentation coming up at school. By recognizing and managing your thoughts, you can turn nervousness into excitement and nail that presentation with confidence!

Or think about making new friends. Understanding how your thoughts and feelings are connected can help you approach new people with a positive mindset, making it easier to form awesome friendships.

Section 1: Cognitive Distortions (CBT)

Understanding Cognitive Distortions

What Are Cognitive Distortions?

Cognitive distortions are like thought habits that our brains develop. They're automatic and often irrational ways of thinking that can mess with our perspective, especially when we're feeling stressed, anxious, or down.

Here are some examples:

1. All-or-Nothing Thinking: This is when you see things in extreme, black-and-white terms, with no middle ground.

- *Example 1: "If I'm not the best player on the team, I'm a total failure."*

- *Example 2: "If I don't get a perfect score on the test, I might as well not bother."*

- *Example 3: "If I can't do this perfectly, there's no point in trying."*

2. Catastrophizing: Catastrophizing is when you blow things way out of proportion.

- *Example 1: "If I trip and fall in front of everyone, my life is ruined."*

- *Example 2: "If I make a mistake during the presentation, I'll never recover from the embarrassment."*

- *Example 3: "If I don't get invited to the party, it means nobody likes me, and I'll be lonely forever."*

3. Mind Reading: Sometimes, our brains make us believe that we can read other people's minds and know exactly what they're thinking.

- *Example 1: "They didn't text me back quickly; they must think I'm annoying."*

- *Example 2: "They looked at me strangely; they must be judging me."*

- *Example 3: "They didn't smile at me today; they must be mad at me."*

4. Should Statements: Should statements are like having a long list of rules in your head.

- *Example 1: "I should always put others' needs before mine."*

- *Example 2: "I should be perfect in everything I do."*

- *Example 3: "I should never ask for help; I should handle everything on my own."*

5. Personalization: When you personalize, you take the blame for everything, even when it's not your fault.

- *Example 1: "My parents are fighting; it must be because of something I did."*

- *Example 2: "My friend is upset; I must have said something to hurt them."*

- *Example 3: "My team lost the game; it's all my fault."*

6. Emotional Reasoning: This one's tricky. It's when you believe that your feelings are facts.

- *Example 1: "I feel stupid, so I must really be stupid."*

- *Example 2: "I feel guilty, so I must have done something wrong."*

- *Example 3: "I feel unlovable, so nobody could possibly care about me."*

Understanding cognitive distortions is like shining a light on these sneaky thought patterns. When you can recognize them, you have the power to challenge and change them, which can make a huge difference in how you feel and how you navigate life's challenges.

With a clearer understanding of what cognitive distortions are, let's dive into "Recognizing Cognitive Distortions" to learn how to spot these tricky thoughts in action.

Recognizing Cognitive Distortions

In the previous section, we talked about what cognitive distortions are and gave you some examples. Now, it's time to become a detective and learn how to recognize these tricky thoughts when they sneak into your mind.

Strategies for Identifying Distorted Thoughts

1. Mindfulness of Thoughts: Mindfulness is your trusty tool here. Start by simply paying attention to your thoughts as they pop up. Imagine your mind as a thought factory, and you're watching the thoughts roll off the assembly line.

2. Keep a Thought Journal: Grab a notebook or use an app to jot down your thoughts when you notice them. This is like taking notes during a detective investigation. Write down what you're thinking, and don't worry if it seems weird or silly at first.

3. Look for Patterns: As you keep your thought journal, you might start seeing patterns. Maybe you notice that you often think in all-or-nothing terms or tend to catastrophize situations. These patterns can be clues that you're dealing with cognitive distortions.

Real-Life Scenarios to Practice Recognition

Let's put your detective skills to the test with some real-life scenarios. See if you can spot the cognitive distortions in action:

Scenario 1: You receive a B on a school assignment, and you think, "I'm such a failure. I should have gotten an A."

Scenario 2: You're waiting for your friend to reply to a message, and they haven't responded for an hour. You think, "They must be ignoring me. They don't want to be friends anymore."

Scenario 3: You make a mistake during a sports game, and you think, "I'm the worst player on the team. I should quit."

Scenario 4: You're preparing for a class presentation, and you think, "I'm going to embarrass myself in front of everyone. I'll forget everything I want to say."

Scenario 5: You're scrolling through social media and see your friends hanging out without you. You think, "They don't like me anymore. I must be boring."

Scenario 6: You're asked to speak in a group discussion, and you think, "Everyone will think my ideas are stupid. I should just stay quiet."

Scenario 7: You have an argument with a family member, and you think, "They hate me now. I'm a terrible sibling/child."

Scenario 8: You have a pimple on your face, and you think, "I look hideous. Nobody will want to talk to me."

Scenario 9: You're not invited to a party, and you think, "I must not be cool enough to hang out with them."

Scenario 10: You don't get the part you wanted in the school play, and you think, "I'm not talented at all. I should never try acting again."

Once you can recognize cognitive distortions in real-life situations, you'll be better equipped to challenge and change them.

Let's move on to the next section, "Challenging Cognitive Distortions," where you'll learn techniques to tackle these tricky thoughts head-on!

Challenging Cognitive Distortions

Now that we've explored what cognitive distortions are and practiced recognizing them in real-life scenarios, it's time to equip you with techniques to challenge and reframe these unhelpful thoughts.

Challenging cognitive distortions isn't about forcing yourself to be unrealistically optimistic. Instead, it's about making tough situations less stressful and more manageable. When you don't challenge these distortions, they can keep you stuck in a cycle of feeling like everything is going wrong, affecting various aspects of your emotional well-being and your interactions with others.

By learning to challenge and reframe your thoughts, you gain the power to break free from this cycle. It doesn't guarantee constant happiness, but it does help you face life's challenges with a clearer and more resilient mindset. It also prevents you from falling into the trap of always feeling like you're in a negative place.

Alright, let's break down why it's super important to challenge those sneaky cognitive distortions.

Imagine This:

You're scrolling through your social media feed, and you see everyone else seemingly having the time of their lives, but wait, you start thinking, "My life is so boring, and I'm just not as cool as them."

Why Does Challenging Cognitive Distortions Matter, You Ask?

1. Keeps You from Feeling Like Crap:

Imagine letting these distorted thoughts take over as you compare yourself to others on social media. Suddenly, you're feeling down, anxious, and just plain yucky. Challenging these thoughts helps prevent that downward spiral, allowing you to maintain a more positive mood and outlook.

2. Improves How You See Yourself:

Now, picture constantly believing you're not good enough compared to the curated images on your feed. These comparisons can make you feel inadequate and inferior, affecting your self-esteem. However, actively challenging these thoughts allows you to see yourself in a more positive light, recognizing your unique strengths and qualities.

3. Better Relationships:

Picture this scenario: you start thinking that your friends secretly don't like you because you're not as exciting as what you see on social media. These thoughts can make you overly self-conscious and anxious, which can strain your relationships. However, by challenging such thoughts, you can alleviate those worries and insecurities, making your relationships smoother and more enjoyable.

4. Less Stress and More Chill:

Life is already full of its own stressors, and you certainly don't need your own thoughts adding to that burden. When you allow distorted thoughts about not measuring up to invade your mind, it can make tough situations feel even more overwhelming. But, when you actively challenge these distortions, it becomes easier to navigate life's challenges with less stress and more composure. It's like finding a calm oasis amid life's chaos.

5. Breaks the Negative Cycle:

Visualize being trapped on a never-ending rollercoaster of negativity, constantly believing these distortions that make you feel inferior and uncool. It's an exhausting and demoralizing cycle. However, when you make the effort to challenge these thoughts, it's like hitting the emergency stop button on that relentless rollercoaster. You can step off the ride and enjoy smoother sailing, free from the perpetual loop of negativity.

So, now that you know why it's crucial, let's dig into some cool strategies to challenge those tricky thoughts. It's like leveling up your mind game, and you've got what it takes to ace it!

Situations, Thoughts, and Emotions

This section helps you identify and document the situations, thoughts, and emotions that trigger your cognitive distortions. Follow these steps:

1. Situation: Start by pinpointing a specific situation or event that triggered the thought, whether related to school, friendships, family, or any aspect of your life.

- ***Example Situation:*** *You had a disagreement with a friend during lunch break.*

2. Thought: Next, write down the exact thought that crossed your mind in response to the situation.

- ***Example Thought:*** *"My friend must hate me now. I'm a terrible friend."*

3. Emotions: Document the emotions you experienced at that moment, which may include sadness, anger, frustration, or worry.

- ***Example Emotions:*** *You felt sad and worried about losing your friend.*

Strategies

This section outlines various strategies to challenge and reframe distorted thoughts. Incorporate these strategies to gain a more balanced perspective:

1. Evidence: Consider whether there is solid proof that your thought is true. Ask yourself if there's concrete evidence to support it. For instance, if you think, "Nobody likes me," reflect on whether you have friends who enjoy spending time with you.

- *Evidence: Your friend has shown care and support before this disagreement, and you've had positive interactions.*

2. Alternative Explanations: Explore alternative explanations for the situation. Could there be other reasons for what you're thinking? Challenge your initial assumptions.

- *Alternative Explanation: Perhaps your friend was having a bad day, and the disagreement wasn't solely about you.*

3. Best Friend Test: Imagine your best friend was in a similar situation and had the same thought. What advice would you give them? Treat yourself with the same kindness and rationality.

- *Advice to a Friend: You might tell your friend that disagreements happen, and it doesn't mean the end of the friendship. Encourage them to talk it out with their friend.*

4. Balanced Thinking: Practice balanced thinking by acknowledging both the positive and negative aspects of the situation. Instead of jumping to extremes, aim for a more middle-ground perspective.

- *Balanced Perspective: While the disagreement was difficult, it doesn't define your entire friendship. There have been many positive moments.*

5. Overgeneralization Challenge: If you notice you're making sweeping statements like "always" or "never," challenge yourself to find exceptions. Are there times when the opposite is true?

- *Challenge to Overgeneralization: Instead of thinking, "I always mess things up," consider the times when you've succeeded or handled situations well.*

6. Mindfulness: Use mindfulness techniques to observe your thoughts without judgment. This can help you detach from distorted thinking and gain a clearer perspective.

- *Mindfulness Practice: Focus on your breath and acknowledge your thoughts without assigning judgment or excessive importance to them.*

7. The Gratitude Exercise: Counter negative thoughts by listing things you're grateful for. This can shift your focus away from distortions and onto positive aspects of your life.

- ***Gratitude List:*** *Write down things you're thankful for, like supportive friends, a loving family, or personal accomplishments.*

8. Seeking Support: Talk to a trusted friend, family member, or therapist about your distorted thoughts. They can provide valuable insights and help you challenge them.

- ***Supportive Conversation:*** *Reach out to a friend and discuss the disagreement, seeking their perspective and advice.*

Remember, challenging cognitive distortions takes practice. Be patient with yourself as you work on changing thought patterns that may have been with you for a while. It's a journey toward more balanced thinking and improved emotional well-being.

Now that you've got these strategies in your toolkit, get ready to put them into action and level up your mind game!

Cognitive Distortions Exploration Worksheet

1. Situation: Recall a recent situation that triggered a strong emotional response.

Sample Response: Last week, I had a disagreement with my best friend.

```
╭────────────────────────────────────────────────────────────────╮
│                                                                  │
│                                                                  │
│                                                                  │
│                                                                  │
╰────────────────────────────────────────────────────────────────╯
```

2. Thought: Write down the thought that occurred during that situation.

Sample Response: I thought, "She must hate me now. Our friendship is over."

```
╭────────────────────────────────────────────────────────────────╮
│                                                                  │
│                                                                  │
│                                                                  │
│                                                                  │
╰────────────────────────────────────────────────────────────────╯
```

3. Emotions: List the emotions you felt as a result of that thought.

Sample Response: I felt sad, anxious, and betrayed.

```
╭────────────────────────────────────────────────────────────────╮
│                                                                  │
│                                                                  │
│                                                                  │
╰────────────────────────────────────────────────────────────────╯
```

4. Identify which cognitive distortion(s) might be present in your thought. Choose from the following common distortions:

- **All-or-Nothing Thinking:** You see things in black-and-white categories with no middle ground.

- **Catastrophizing:** You expect the worst possible outcome.

- **Filtering:** You focus exclusively on the negative aspects of a situation.

- **Overgeneralization:** You see a single negative event as a never-ending pattern.

- **Personalization:** You believe everything people do or say is a reaction to you.

• **Mind Reading:** You believe you know what others are thinking and assume it's negative.

Sample Response: In this thought, I can see both "Catastrophizing" and "Mind Reading." I'm assuming the worst outcome (catastrophizing), and I'm thinking I know exactly what my friend is thinking (mind reading).

5. Recognizing Cognitive Distortions

Now, for the thought you've identified, explain which cognitive distortion(s) you think might be present. Provide a brief explanation for each distortion you've identified.

Sample Response:

• **Catastrophizing:** *I'm jumping to the worst possible conclusion - that our entire friendship is over because of one disagreement.*

• **Mind Reading:** *I'm assuming I know what my friend is thinking without any evidence.*

6. Challenging Cognitive Distortions

Challenge the thought by asking yourself these questions:

A. Is there solid evidence that supports this thought?

Provide evidence that either supports or contradicts your initial thought.

Sample Response: There's no solid evidence that our entire friendship is over. We've had disagreements before and always worked things out.

B. What would you say to a friend who had this thought in a similar situation?

Imagine a friend experienced the same situation and had the same thought. What supportive and balanced advice would you offer them?

Sample Response: I would tell my friend that one disagreement doesn't mean the end of a friendship. It's important to talk things out and understand each other's perspectives.

7. Reframe the Thought

After considering the evidence and advice for a friend, reframe your initial thought into a more balanced and realistic one.

Sample Response: "We had a disagreement, but that doesn't mean our whole friendship is ruined. I should talk to her and try to understand her point of view."

8. Practice Reflection

Write down your reframed thought and reflect on how this exercise helped you gain a better understanding of your thought patterns and cognitive distortions.

Sample Response: My reframed thought is, "We had a disagreement, but that doesn't mean our whole friendship is ruined. I should talk to her and try to understand her point of view." This exercise made me realize that my initial thought was an overreaction, and I need to communicate with my friend to resolve the issue.

Section 2: Emotional Regulation (DBT)

In Section 1, we examined how thoughts and feelings are interconnected, shedding light on cognitive distortions through the lens of Cognitive Behavioral Therapy (CBT). Now, in Section 2, we venture into the world of emotions, guided by Dialectical Behavior Therapy (DBT). This section explores the profound role emotions play in shaping our thoughts and behaviors, offering a distinct perspective from CBT.

The Role of Emotions: A DBT Perspective

Emotions are like the colorful threads that weave the fabric of our lives. They're not just random feelings that come and go; they play a crucial role in how we think, act, and interact with the world around us. In this section, we'll explore the profound significance of emotions, particularly from the perspective of Dialectical Behavior Therapy (DBT).

Exploring the Purpose of Emotions

Emotions aren't just there to make you laugh, cry, or feel excited. They serve a much deeper purpose. Think of them as your body's way of communicating with you, like an internal messaging system. Emotions convey important information about your experiences and help you navigate the complexities of life.

Imagine you're in a dark forest, and suddenly you hear a rustling noise behind you. Your heart starts racing, and you feel a surge of fear. That fear is your body's way of saying, "Hey, something's not right here! Be alert, and stay safe!" Emotions like fear are designed to prepare you for action and protect you from potential threats.

How Emotions Influence Thoughts and Behaviors

Emotions aren't isolated experiences; they have a significant impact on your thoughts and behaviors. When you're feeling happy, you're more likely to have positive thoughts and engage in activities that bring you joy. On the other hand, when you're angry, your thoughts might become more negative, and you might act impulsively.

For example, if you're excited about a project, you're more likely to think creatively and work diligently on it. But if you're feeling anxious, your thoughts might become scattered, and you might procrastinate. Emotions can either fuel your productivity or hinder it, depending on what you're feeling.

What Emotions Are NOT

Emotions are powerful, but they're not all-knowing. They don't provide absolute truths or facts about the world. Emotions are subjective, and they can be influenced by various factors, including past experiences, beliefs, and personal interpretations. It's essential to remember that while emotions offer valuable information, they don't always paint a complete picture of reality.

Sitch 1: Coffee date

Imagine you're waiting to meet a friend for a coffee date, and your friend is running late. You start feeling anxious, thinking, "They must not care about our friendship anymore; that's why they're late." Your anxiety and thoughts begin to spiral, and you feel hurt and upset.

In this scenario, your emotions are telling you that you're anxious, hurt, and upset. However, what emotions are not in this situation is an absolute truth or a fact that your friend no longer cares about your friendship. Emotions can be influenced by your past experiences, personal insecurities, and interpretations of the situation. It's essential to recognize that your emotional response doesn't necessarily reflect the objective reality of your friend's feelings or intentions. Emotions, in this case, are a subjective response to the situation rather than an undeniable fact.

Sitch 2: Tough Test Day at School

Picture this: It's a major test day at school, and you've been studying super hard. But as you sit down to take the test, your mind goes blank, and you start panicking. You think, "I'm gonna fail this test, and my life is ruined!" Your emotions start racing, and you feel totally stressed out.

But here's what's real, in this sitch, your emotions are screaming that you're stressed and freaked out. But what they're not saying is that it's like, 100% set in stone that you're gonna fail the test and your life is over. Emotions can be fueled by the pressure of the moment, past test worries, and how you're seeing the situation right then. So, even though you're dealing with a bunch of feels, it doesn't mean it's all over. Emotions are more about how you're handling things at that moment, not a final verdict on your future.

Sitch 3: Family Dinner Drama

Now, think about this: You're at a family dinner, and there's some drama going on. Maybe there's an argument, or someone's upset about something. You start feeling super uncomfortable and think, "My family is falling apart, and it's all my fault." Your emotions get all tangled up, and you feel guilty and sad.

But here's the scoop, in this sitch, your emotions are telling you that you're guilty and sad. But what they're not saying is that it's, like, totally true that your family is falling apart and it's all on you. Emotions can get stirred up by family stuff, past experiences, and how you're interpreting the situation. So, even though you're caught up in those emotions, it doesn't mean you're the one responsible for everything. Emotions here are more about how you're reacting in the moment, not a final judgment on your family.

Emotions as Messengers: A DBT Distinction

In the world of therapy, different approaches offer unique perspectives on emotions. Here's where Dialectical Behavior Therapy (DBT) stands out, diverging from Cognitive Behavioral Therapy (CBT) in its viewpoint.

DBT places a strong emphasis on understanding emotions as messengers. It sees emotions not as mere reactions but as vital messages from your inner world. Each emotion, like a colored flag, signifies something specific. Just as you'd respond differently to different flag colors, you can learn to respond effectively to various emotions.

For instance, imagine sadness as a blue flag, waving to let you know about a loss or the need for self-care. Anger, on the other hand, might be a red flag signaling a boundary violation or a need to assert yourself.

In contrast, CBT primarily focuses on the connection between thoughts, feelings, and behaviors. It explores how distorted thoughts can lead to negative emotions and behaviors. While CBT is valuable, DBT extends this understanding by highlighting the importance of recognizing emotions as unique messengers, offering insights into our inner experiences.

In the upcoming sections, we'll delve deeper into how to manage and regulate your emotions effectively using DBT techniques. Learning to decipher these emotional messages and respond to them in a healthy way is a crucial skill for a happier and more balanced life.

Let's journey further into the world of emotions and discover practical DBT strategies to navigate them effectively.

Understanding Emotions Worksheet

Part 1: Recognizing Emotions

1. Situation: Think of a recent situation that triggered strong emotions for you.

- *Sample Response 1: During a school presentation, I couldn't remember my lines, and my mind went blank.*

- *Sample Response 2: When I received a rejection email after a job interview I was really excited about.*

- *Sample Response 3: When my best friend canceled our plans at the last minute.*

- *Sample Response 4: After I missed my bus and was running late for an important meeting.*

- *Sample Response 5: When I saw a stray dog shivering in the cold outside my house.*

2. Primary Emotion: Identify the primary emotion you experienced in that situation.

- *Sample Response 1: I felt extremely anxious during the presentation.*

- *Sample Response 2: I felt deeply disappointed after the job interview rejection.*

- *Sample Response 3: I was frustrated and a bit hurt when my friend canceled our plans.*

- *Sample Response 4: I was overwhelmed by stress because I was running late.*

- *Sample Response 5: I felt a strong sense of empathy and concern for the stray dog.*

3. Thoughts and Behaviors: Reflect on the thoughts and behaviors that accompanied this emotion.

- *Sample Response 1: My thoughts were racing, and I felt like everyone was judging me. I stumbled over my words and felt embarrassed.*

- *Sample Response 2: I thought I had failed the interview miserably, and I started doubting my skills and qualifications. I spent the day feeling down and reevaluating my career choices.*

- *Sample Response 3: I thought my friend didn't value our plans, and I felt like she was being inconsiderate. I ended up watching TV alone and feeling a bit lonely.*

- *Sample Response 4: My thoughts were chaotic, and I was worried about the consequences of being late. I rushed and forgot some important documents for the meeting.*

- *Sample Response 5: I couldn't stop thinking about the dog and how I could help. I ended up bringing it inside and calling an animal shelter.*

Part 2: The Purpose of Emotions

4. Emotional Message: Consider what the emotion you identified was trying to communicate to you. Why did you feel this way in that situation?

- *Sample Response 1: The anxiety I felt during the presentation was trying to communicate that I cared about doing well in front of my peers. It was signaling that I needed to practice more and build my confidence in public speaking.*

- *Sample Response 2: The disappointment after the job interview rejection was trying to communicate that I had high hopes for that opportunity. It was signaling that I should keep searching for a job that aligns with my aspirations.*

- *Sample Response 3: The frustration and hurt when my friend canceled plans were trying to communicate that I value our time together. It was signaling that I should express my feelings and discuss the importance of our plans.*

- *Sample Response 4: The stress from running late for the meeting was trying to communicate the importance of punctuality. It was signaling that I should manage my time better to avoid such situations.*

- *Sample Response 5: The empathy and concern for the stray dog were trying to communicate my compassion for animals in need. It was signaling that I should take action to help the dog and possibly consider supporting animal welfare causes.*

> (empty rounded box)

5. Benefit of Understanding: Explain how understanding the message behind your emotion can be beneficial for you.

- *Sample Response 1:* *By understanding that my anxiety was linked to my desire for improvement, I can work on my public speaking skills, which will benefit me in future presentations.*

- *Sample Response 2:* *Understanding that my disappointment stemmed from high expectations allows me to adjust my job search strategy and stay motivated in my career journey.*

- *Sample Response 3:* *Recognizing the value of our plans and addressing my feelings with my friend can lead to more open communication and stronger friendships.*

- *Sample Response 4:* *Acknowledging the importance of punctuality can help me develop better time management habits, reducing stress in the long run.*

- *Sample Response 5:* *Acting on my empathy and concern for the stray dog not only helped the animal but also reinforced my commitment to supporting causes I care about.*

> (empty rounded box)

Emotional Regulation Strategies

Emotions are a natural and vital aspect of our humanity, especially during your teenage years. However, they can occasionally become overwhelming or challenging to manage. In this section, we'll explore practical techniques and Dialectical Behavior Therapy (DBT) skills that can empower you to effectively manage intense emotions.

Practical Techniques for You

Mindfulness

Time for a little refresher from Chapter 1! Remember the awesome technique called mindfulness? It's a total game-changer when it comes to handling your emotions. This trick is all about staying fully in the moment, no judgment allowed. With mindfulness, you get to observe your thoughts and feelings as they happen, giving you the upper hand to respond thoughtfully instead of reacting on impulse.

Emotion Labeling

Accurately identifying and labeling your emotions is a fundamental skill for emotional regulation. When you can name your feelings, you gain better control over them and can take appropriate action. Here's a detailed step-by-step guide on how to practice emotion labeling:

1. Self-Reflection: Find a quiet and comfortable place where you can sit and reflect on your emotions. It's essential to create a safe space where you can be honest with yourself.

2. Close Your Eyes: If it helps you focus, you can close your eyes. This step is optional but can be beneficial in reducing distractions.

3. Take a Deep Breath: Begin by taking a few slow, deep breaths to center yourself and create a sense of calm.

4. Identify Your Emotion: Now, think about the emotion you're currently experiencing. It might be a single emotion or a combination of several. Try to pinpoint it as accurately as possible. For example, you might be feeling "frustrated," "disappointed," or "anxious."

5. Use an Emotion List: If you're having trouble identifying your emotion, you can refer to the emotion list in Appendix A. This list contains a range of emotions, and you can choose the ones that best describe what you're feeling. This can expand your emotional vocabulary and help you pinpoint your emotions more precisely.

6. Acknowledge Without Judgment: Once you've identified your emotion, acknowledge it without judgment. Emotions are neither good nor bad; they're natural responses to our experiences. It's okay to feel the way you do.

7. Reflect on the Trigger: Take a moment to reflect on what triggered this emotion. Was it a specific event, interaction, or thought? Understanding the source of your emotion can provide valuable insights into your inner world.

8. Consider the Intensity: Assess the intensity of your emotion on a scale from 1 to 10, with 1 being barely noticeable and 10 being extremely intense. This can help you gauge the significance of what you're feeling.

9. Plan Your Response: Depending on the emotion you've identified and its intensity, consider how you want to respond. Is there a specific action you can take to address the emotion, or do you simply need to allow yourself to feel it without immediate action?

10. Practice Regularly: Emotion labeling is a skill that becomes more refined with practice. Make it a habit to check in with your emotions regularly, especially during moments of stress or heightened feelings.

Practice Exercise: Here's a simple exercise to get you started. Set aside a few minutes each day for emotion labeling. Sit in a quiet space, close your eyes if you prefer, and take a few deep breaths. Reflect on your current emotions and use an emotion list if needed. Identify and label your emotions, acknowledging them without judgment. Consider what triggered these feelings and plan your response accordingly. Over time, this practice will help you become more in tune with your emotions and better equipped to manage them.

Distress Tolerance

Distress tolerance skills, a fundamental component of Dialectical Behavior Therapy (DBT), are designed to assist you in managing overwhelming emotions as they arise. These skills serve as a buffer against impulsive reactions and provide a valuable sense of control. Here's an in-depth guide on how to employ distress tolerance skills effectively:

1. Understanding Distress Tolerance: Begin by understanding the concept of distress tolerance. Recognize that these skills are not about eliminating emotions but rather about managing them in challenging situations. Distress tolerance skills help you ride the waves of intense emotions without getting swept away by them.

2. Identify Your Emotional Triggers: Pay attention to situations, people, or circumstances that trigger intense emotions in you. Identifying your emotional triggers allows you to prepare for potential distressing situations.

3. Learn Distress Tolerance Techniques: Explore various distress tolerance techniques, such as the TIPP skill. TIPP stands for Temperature, Intense exercise, Paced breathing, and Paired muscle relaxation. Each of these techniques can be used to create a physical sensation that helps distract you from overwhelming emotions.

4. Practice the TIPP Skill: Specifically, focus on learning and practicing the TIPP skill. When faced with an emotionally charged situation where impulsive reactions are likely, follow these steps:

- **Temperature:** Have a cold pack, ice cube, or a bowl of cold water ready.

- **Intense Exercise:** Engage in a brief, intense physical activity like jumping jacks or running in place.

- **Paced Breathing:** Practice deep breathing exercises, inhaling for a count of four, holding for four, and exhaling for four.

- **Paired Muscle Relaxation:** Pair muscle tensing and releasing to create a relaxing sensation. For example, tense your muscles for a few seconds and then release them.

5. Choose the Most Effective Technique: Depending on the situation and your personal preferences, select the distress tolerance technique that is most effective for you. Experiment with each technique to determine which one works best in different circumstances.

6. Prevent Impulsive Reactions: The primary goal of distress tolerance skills is to prevent impulsive reactions that may lead to regret or negative consequences. By applying these skills, you can regain emotional control, think more clearly, and make informed decisions.

7. Build Resilience: As you practice distress tolerance skills, you will gradually build emotional resilience. Over time, you'll become better equipped to handle distressing situations without becoming overwhelmed.

Practice Exercise: Learn and practice the TIPP skill, focusing on the Temperature component. Keep a cold pack or ice cube readily available. The next time you encounter a highly distressing situation, apply the TIPP skill by holding the cold pack or ice cube for a short period. Notice how this physical sensation helps distract you from the intensity of your emotions and allows you to regain control.

Emotion Regulation Worksheet: A Step-by-Step Guide

Emotions can be complex and sometimes overwhelming. The Emotion Regulation Worksheet combines the skills you learned above to help you understand, manage, and regulate your emotions effectively. This worksheet guides you through a structured process to gain insights into your emotional experiences and develop strategies for coping with them.

Step 1: Identifying Emotions

In this step, you identify and name the specific emotions you are experiencing. Emotions are complex, and sometimes, you may feel more than one at a time. It's essential to accurately label your emotions to gain a better understanding of how you're feeling.

- *Sample Response 1:* *"I am feeling happy and excited.*

- *Sample Response 2:* *"I am feeling anxious and overwhelmed."*

- *Sample Response 3:* *"I am feeling sad and lonely."*

- *Sample Response 4:* *"I am feeling irritated and impatient."*

- *Sample Response 5:* *"I am feeling calm and content."*

Step 2: Understanding Triggers

Identifying what triggered your emotions is crucial for emotional regulation. Triggers can be events, situations, thoughts, or interactions that set off your emotional response. Understanding these triggers helps you gain insight into the source of your emotions.

- *Sample Response 1:* *"These emotions were triggered when I received good news about a job offer."*

- *Sample Response 2:* *"The trigger for these emotions was a stressful presentation at work."*

- *Sample Response 3:* *"I felt sad and lonely because I saw a photo of friends hanging out without me on social media."*

- *Sample Response 4:* *"My impatience and irritation were triggered by a long wait in traffic."*

- *Sample Response 5:* *"I became anxious and overwhelmed when I had a disagreement with a family member."*

Step 3: Physical Sensations

Emotions often manifest physically in our bodies. This step encourages you to notice and describe any physical sensations you experience when feeling the identified emotions. Paying attention to physical sensations can help you connect with your emotions on a deeper level.

- *Sample Response 1:* *"I noticed a warm, joyful feeling in my chest."*

- *Sample Response 2:* *"I felt a knot in my stomach and my palms were sweaty."*

- *Sample Response 3:* *"My heart started racing, and I had a lump in my throat."*

- *Sample Response 4:* *"I experienced a tension headache and shallow breathing."*

- *Sample Response 5:* *"My body felt relaxed and at ease."*

Step 4: Thoughts and Beliefs

Our thoughts and beliefs strongly influence our emotions. In this step, you describe the thoughts and beliefs that accompanied your emotions. These thoughts often provide insight into why you are feeling a certain way.

- *Sample Response 1:* *"I thought about all the opportunities this job offer would bring."*

- *Sample Response 2:* *"I believed that my performance during the presentation would determine my career success."*

- *Sample Response 3:* *"I thought my friends didn't want to include me because they find me boring."*

- *Sample Response 4:* *"I believed that the traffic jam was a waste of my time."*

- *Sample Response 5:* *"I thought that my family member was being unfair and unreasonable."*

Step 5: Behaviors and Actions

Emotions can drive our behaviors and actions. Here, you describe how you acted or what you did in response to your emotions. Recognizing your behaviors helps you see how emotions impact your actions.

- *Sample Response 1:* *"I celebrated by going out for dinner with friends."*

- *Sample Response 2:* *"I procrastinated and avoided preparing for the presentation."*

- *Sample Response 3:* *"I withdrew from social interactions and spent time alone."*

- *Sample Response 4:* *"I honked my horn and changed lanes aggressively in traffic."*

- *Sample Response 5:* *"I argued loudly with my family member and left the room."*

By going through these steps, you gain a comprehensive understanding of your emotions and their underlying causes. This awareness is the first step in effectively managing and regulating your emotions.

Opposite Action Worksheet

When your emotions are driving you to engage in unhelpful behaviors, the skill of opposite action teaches you to do the opposite of what your initial impulse suggests. This technique can lead to a change in emotions and more constructive outcomes. Here's a comprehensive guide on how to apply opposite action effectively:

1. Identify the Situation and Emotions: Pay attention to the emotions you're experiencing in a particular situation. For example, if you're feeling fear or anxiety, acknowledge these emotions.

- **Sample Response:** *I'm staring at this huge pile of work that needs to be done, and just thinking about starting it makes me feel all uneasy and restless. I know these feelings mean I'm procrastinating again. I gotta admit, I'm totally avoiding getting started on this task.*

2. Recognize Your Initial Impulse: Identify the impulsive behaviors or actions that your emotions might prompt you to take. These actions may not be in your best interest or may lead to negative consequences.

- **Sample Response:** *When I'm faced with a big assignment, my first instinct is to put it off, even though I know it's not the best idea and could end up causing problems.*

3. Recognizing the Potential for Opposite Action: Acknowledge how opposite action can help in challenging situations.

- **Sample Response:** *I know that taking the opposite action can actually lead to good stuff. So, even though my first instinct is to put off the task, if I start it now, I'll have more time later for things I really love doing once it's done.*

4. Choose and practice the Opposite Response: Deliberately choose a response that is the opposite of your initial impulse and put it into action. If your initial impulse is to procrastinate, opt for a response that involves starting your study session.

- *Sample Response: Instead of letting procrastination take over, I'm gonna do the opposite by setting a timer for a quick study session, even if it's just 15 minutes.*

5. Observe and Reflect on the Outcome: Take note of how implementing opposite action impacts both your emotions and the overall situation. Reflect on whether it leads to more positive interactions and changes in your emotional state.

- *Sample Response: At first, I totally didn't feel like studying, but I pushed myself to start anyway. And you know what? Once I got into it, my mood actually got better, and I felt more focused. Taking that opposite action really paid off - not only did I get stuff done, but I also felt way better about it.*

6. Apply Opposite Action Mindfully: Continue practicing opposite action in various situations. Over time, you'll develop the skill of choosing responses that align with your long-term goals and values rather than impulsive reactions driven by intense emotions. Look for opportunities to apply opposite action in other areas of your life, such as tackling challenges or confronting fears with a proactive approach.

Roleplay Activity - Trying New Food

Imagine you usually avoid trying new foods because you're not sure if you'll like them. This avoidance is driven by a feeling of discomfort or anxiety about the unknown. In this roleplay activity, challenge yourself to apply opposite action. Choose to try a new food, even if you're feeling hesitant or unsure.

1. Identify the Emotion: Recognize the emotion you're experiencing, which, in this case, may be anxiety or discomfort about trying something new.

2. Recognize the Initial Impulse: Acknowledge your initial impulse to decline trying the new food because it's unfamiliar.

3. Recognizing the Potential for Opposite Action: Stepping out of your comfort zone might lead to discovering some lit flavors and experiences. So, instead of passing, consider saying yes to the adventure.

4. Choose and Practice the Opposite Action: Decide to try the new food, even if you want to say no at first. Step out of your comfort zone and give it a shot. Taste a small bit, really noticing the flavors and textures.

5. Observation and Reflection: As you take a bite of the new food, notice how choosing to try it despite your initial discomfort affects your emotions. Reflect on how your experience of trying the new food changes as a result of this decision. Consider whether this choice shifts your perception of trying new things and how it might influence your future willingness to step out of your comfort zone.

7. Apply Opposite Action Mindfully: Consider how you can apply the concept of opposite action in other areas of your life when facing situations that challenge your comfort zone.

By completing this roleplay activity, you can gain a firsthand understanding of how opposite action can lead to positive outcomes and help you manage your emotions effectively.

Radical Acceptance Worksheet

Sometimes, it's essential to accept that certain situations or emotions cannot be changed. Radical acceptance helps you find peace in these moments.

Radical Acceptance is a crucial skill for accepting situations or emotions that cannot be changed. It helps you find inner peace and cope with challenging moments. Here's a comprehensive guide on how to practice Radical Acceptance:

1. Identify the Situation and Emotion: Recognize the specific situation or emotion that you're struggling to accept. It could be a personal setback, a loss, or a challenging emotion like grief.

- *Sample Response: When I see a low test grade, my initial emotion is disappointment.*

2. Acknowledge Your Resistance: Understand that resistance to the situation or emotion is natural. You may initially want to deny or avoid it, but Radical Acceptance encourages you to acknowledge your resistance.

- *Sample Response: I realize that I initially wish I had done better on the test and feel upset about the grade.*

3. Recognize the Radical Acceptance Potential: Consider how Radical Acceptance could assist in this scenario. Instead of resisting, it encourages facing tough situations or feelings. By accepting the reality of the situation and your emotions, you might discover inner peace and strength.

- *Sample Response: So, I get a bad grade. Instead of freaking out, I gotta deal with it and move on. Accepting it helps me figure out what to improve for next time.*

[blank rounded text box]

4. Choose and Practice Radical Acceptance: Make a conscious choice to practice Radical Acceptance. Decide to fully accept the situation or emotion, knowing that resisting it will only cause more suffering. Allow yourself to experience it without judgment or attempts to change it.

- ***Sample Response:*** *I choose to accept the low test grade and my feelings of disappointment and frustration. I embrace the reality of the situation without dwelling on what could have been.*

[blank rounded text box]

5. Observation and Reflection: Observe how practicing Radical Acceptance impacts your emotional state and your ability to navigate challenging situations or emotions. Then, take some time to reflect on how this approach allows you to respond with greater peace and effectiveness.

- ***Sample Response:*** *As I practice Radical Acceptance, I notice how I feel when I get a bad grade. Instead of spiraling, I accept it. I'll feel better and less stressed. Then I'll think about what I could do better next time. It's like, okay, I got this, let's learn from it.*

[blank rounded text box]

6. Apply Radical Acceptance in Life: Look for opportunities to practice Radical Acceptance in other aspects of your life when faced with situations or emotions that cannot be changed. Recognize that this skill can lead to greater emotional resilience. Apply Radical Acceptance to other challenges you encounter, such as accepting a traffic delay instead of getting frustrated.

Roleplay Activity - Embracing a Rainy Day:

Imagine you had planned a fun outdoor event with friends, and you were looking forward to it. However, on the day of the event, it starts pouring rain, and your plans are ruined. In this roleplay activity, practice Radical Acceptance by embracing the situation without resistance.

1. Identify the Situation: Recognize the situation of the rainy day, which prevents your outdoor event from taking place.

2. Recognize the Radical Acceptance Potential: Instead of dwelling on the situation, Radical Acceptance can help me think about solutions and how to make the best of of my situation.

3. Acknowledge Your Resistance: Acknowledge any feelings of disappointment, frustration, or annoyance that arise due to the rain.

4. Choose and Practice Radical Acceptance: Choose to practice Radical Acceptance by fully accepting the rainy day and the change of plans. Embrace it mindfully by finding an alternative indoor activity or simply enjoying the rain without wishing it were different.

5. Observation and Reflection: Notice how accepting the rainy day affects your mood and your readiness to adapt to the indoor plans. Reflect on how embracing the unexpected weather enables you to make the most of the situation and still enjoy quality time with friends indoors, despite the change in plans.

6. Apply Radical Acceptance in Life: Consider how you can apply Radical Acceptance to other unexpected situations that may arise in the future.

By engaging in this roleplay activity, you can gain valuable insights into the practice of Radical Acceptance and its potential to bring peace and resilience in the face of life's challenges.

Self-Soothe Worksheet

Self-Soothe is a skill that empowers you to engage in soothing activities or create comfort kits when you're facing intense emotions. It's a valuable tool for calming yourself and finding emotional relief. Here's a comprehensive guide on how to practice Self-Soothe:

1. Identify the Situation and Intense Emotions: Recognize when you're experiencing intense emotions. It could be feelings of stress, anxiety, sadness, or anger.

- *Sample Response: So, I'm feeling mega stressed out because of all the school stuff and drama with friends. It's like, everything's piling up, you know?*

2. Recognizing Self-Soothing Potential: Consider how engaging in self-soothing activities can help manage intense emotions. Instead of being overwhelmed, recognize the power of calming techniques to bring comfort and relief.

- *Sample Response: Instead of letting school stress and drama get to me, I'm trying to find ways to chill. I love blasting my favorite tunes and making a playlist that just calms me down. It's like my go-to for when things get crazy, and it really helps me feel more in control.*

3. Select Soothing Activities: Choose soothing activities that bring you comfort and help alleviate your intense emotions. These activities can vary from person to person and may include reading, listening to calming music, taking a warm bath, or practicing deep breathing exercises.

- *Sample Response:* I've decided to take a break and do something soothing, like listening to my favorite tunes and putting together a playlist that just relaxes me. It's like my way of escaping the chaos for a bit and finding some peace.

4. Create a Comfort Kit: If you prefer a physical approach, create a comfort kit that contains items that bring you comfort and joy. It could include items like a soft blanket, scented candles, a favorite book, or a stress-relief toy.

- *Sample Response:* I'm putting together this comfort kit with stuff like a cozy blanket, some scented candles, and a journal to jot down how I'm feeling. It's like having my own little safe space to chill out and unwind whenever I need it.

5. Set Aside Time: Dedicate a specific time to engage in your chosen soothing activity or use your comfort kit. Setting aside time ensures that you prioritize self-soothing during moments of distress.

- *Sample Response: I've set aside 20 minutes before bedtime to just unwind and listen to my calming music playlist. It's become this nightly ritual that helps me relax and clear my mind before hitting the hay.*

6. Observing and Reflecting on Self-Soothing: Take a moment to observe how engaging in self-soothing activities impacts your emotional state. Afterward, reflect on how this practice aids in managing intense emotions and finding emotional relief.

- *Sample Response: By diving into calming music and my comfort kit, I can feel this wave of calm and relaxation wash over me. It's like these activities have become my go-to tools for dealing with stress and just feeling better overall. It's amazing how something as simple as a cozy blanket and some soothing tunes can make such a big difference in how I feel.*

By learning these emotional regulation strategies and DBT skills, you empower yourself to navigate the ups and downs of adolescence with greater resilience and emotional well-being. These tools can help you develop lifelong skills for managing emotions and building a brighter future.

Emotional Resilience: Building Strength for Life's Challenges

Emotional resilience is like having an inner superpower that helps you face life's ups and downs with confidence. It's important to know that it doesn't just happen magically; it's part of growing up and developing as a person. So, don't worry if you're still working on it – that's completely normal!

Now, let's dive into real-life stories that show how emotional resilience can help you handle all kinds of challenges like a champ. These case studies will give you a sneak peek into how emotional resilience can make your life better in so many ways.

Case Study 1: Friendship - Building Emotional Resilience

The Challenge:

Jenna had a best friend, Mia, since they were little kids. They did everything together, but as they grew older, they started having more disagreements and fights. One day, they had a big argument that led to a major falling out. Jenna felt hurt and angry. She thought their friendship was over.

Non-Resilient Reaction:

Non-resilience in this situation might look like Jenna completely shutting down emotionally. She might avoid talking to Mia or refuse to consider trying to mend the friendship. Jenna could be stuck in her anger and sadness, unable to see a way forward.

Emotionally Resilient Response:

Instead of giving up on the friendship, Jenna decided to be emotionally resilient. She took a step back to calm her feelings and decided to talk to Mia about what happened. Jenna was open to understanding Mia's perspective and expressing her own feelings. Through open communication and compromise, they found a way to rebuild their friendship even stronger than before.

Outcome:

Jenna's emotional resilience helped her navigate the rocky road of friendship. She learned that disagreements and misunderstandings happen, but they don't have to be the end. Jenna and Mia's friendship became more resilient, and they learned valuable lessons about communication and understanding.

Case Study 2: School - Building Emotional Resilience

The Challenge:

Alex was a high school student who struggled with keeping up with assignments and exams. He often felt overwhelmed by the workload and feared getting bad grades. This stress led to sleepless nights and anxiety.

Non-Resilient Reaction:

A non-resilient reaction for Alex would be avoiding his schoolwork altogether. He might procrastinate, skip classes, or give up on assignments. This would only increase his stress and anxiety.

Emotionally Resilient Response:

Alex decided to build emotional resilience. He recognized that school challenges wouldn't disappear, so he needed to tackle them head-on. Alex began by breaking down his tasks into manageable steps, using problem-solving skills he learned earlier. He also reached out to a teacher for help and started a study group with friends. This proactive approach helped him regain control and manage his stress better.

Outcome:

By building emotional resilience, Alex not only improved his grades but also gained a sense of accomplishment and confidence. He learned that facing challenges and seeking help when needed were essential skills for a successful school life.

Case Study 3: Family - Building Emotional Resilience

The Challenge:

Sophie's family was going through a tough time. Her parents were always arguing and considering divorce. Sophie felt like her world was falling apart, and she didn't know how to handle the constant tension at home.

Non-Resilient Reaction:

A non-resilient response for Sophie could be withdrawing from her family entirely. She might avoid family gatherings, ignore the problems, or isolate herself in her room. This would only lead to more emotional turmoil.

Emotionally Resilient Response:

Sophie decided to build emotional resilience by acknowledging her feelings and seeking support. She talked to her parents about how their arguments were affecting her, and they started family counseling. Sophie also connected with a school counselor and joined a support group for teens going through similar family challenges. She learned that facing her emotions and seeking help were strengths, not weaknesses.

Outcome:

Building emotional resilience helped Sophie and her family navigate a difficult time. Through therapy and open communication, Sophie's parents began to work on their issues, and the family environment gradually improved. Sophie realized that facing challenges and seeking help were essential for her and her family's well-being.

Section 3: Understanding Personal Values

In the previous section, we delved into the intricate relationship between thoughts and emotions, exploring how cognitive distortions can cloud our perceptions and how emotional regulation strategies can help us manage intense feelings. Now, as we move forward, we shift our focus towards a different aspect of holistic therapy – values and commitment, a core component of Acceptance and Commitment Therapy (ACT).

While Cognitive Behavioral Therapy (CBT) and Dialectical Behavior Therapy (DBT) primarily concentrate on identifying and challenging cognitive distortions and regulating emotions, ACT takes a slightly different route. In ACT, we recognize the profound impact of personal values on our lives.

Understanding Personal Values

Defining Personal Values: Personal values are like your life's GPS – they show you the way to what truly matters. Imagine them as your unique map, guiding you toward what's important and meaningful to you. They're like your inner compass, helping you decide what feels genuinely right.

By understanding your personal values, you're unlocking a powerful tool that can keep you grounded and stable, especially when life throws curveballs your way.

Here are some examples of personal values to give you an idea:

- **Kindness:** Imagine you have a core value of kindness. You go out of your way to help a friend who's feeling down, and it brings a warm feeling to your heart. That's because your actions align with your value, and it makes you feel like you're being your best self.

- **Creativity:** Let's say creativity is one of your values. When you spend time drawing or painting, you feel a deep sense of satisfaction and joy. It's because you're expressing your true self and honoring your value for creativity.

- **Honesty:** If honesty is a value you hold dear, you're known for your integrity among your friends. People trust you, and your relationships are built on a strong foundation of honesty.

- **Adventure:** Adventure might be one of your values. When you plan an exciting road trip with friends, you feel alive and invigorated. Embracing adventure fulfills your sense of exploration and curiosity.

Self-Reflection Exercises to Identify Core Values

Okay, so you might be wondering, "How do I figure out what my values are?" Well, that's where self-reflection comes in!

Self-Reflection: Self-reflection means taking some quiet time to think deeply about yourself and your experiences. In this part of the chapter, we're going to guide you through some fun and thought-provoking exercises to help you identify your core values.

Exercise 1: What Activities Make You Feel Most Alive?

1. Take a moment to think about the activities or hobbies that make you feel genuinely excited and alive. It could be anything from playing a musical instrument to hiking in nature or volunteering at a local shelter.

- *Sample Response:* *"I feel most alive when I'm playing my guitar. The music just flows through me, and I lose track of time."*

2. Write down at least three activities that come to mind and describe how they make you feel. What is it about these activities that ignite a spark in you?

- *Sample Response:* *"I also love hiking in the mountains. Being surrounded by nature gives me a sense of peace and freedom. It's like a reset button for my soul."*

Exercise 2: What Kind of People Do You Admire?

1. Think about the people you look up to and admire in your life. They could be family members, friends, celebrities, or historical figures. What qualities or characteristics do they possess that you find inspiring?

- *Sample Response:* *"I admire my grandma because she's incredibly compassionate and always there to help others in need. She's a true role model."*

2. List at least three people you admire and write down the qualities or values that you find most appealing about them.

- *Sample Response:* *"I also admire Gitanjali Rao for her innovation and determination. She's constantly pushing boundaries and thinking outside the box."*

Exercise 3: Journaling Prompts

1. Grab your journal and answer the following prompts: "When I imagine my ideal life, what am I doing, and who am I surrounded by?"

- *Sample Response:* "In my ideal life, I'm working as a marine biologist, studying and protecting the ocean. I'm surrounded by a supportive and adventurous group of friends who share my passion."

2. "What causes or issues in the world do I care deeply about?"

- *Sample Response:* "I deeply care about environmental conservation and animal welfare. These causes resonate with me because I believe in taking care of our planet and all its creatures."

Core Values Worksheet

Now, it's time to delve deeper into discovering your core values with the Core Values Worksheet. This worksheet is designed to help you rank and prioritize your values based on your responses to the previous exercises. By the end of this exercise, you'll have a clear sense of what truly matters to you and what values define who you are.

1. List Your Values: Begin by listing the values that resonated with you during the self-reflection exercises. You can use the responses from the previous exercises as a starting point. You can find a list of values in Appendix B.

- *Sample Response: "Based on my reflections, some of the values that matter to me include creativity, compassion, adventure, and environmental stewardship."*

2. Rank Your Values: Now, take a moment to rank these values from most important (1) to least important (4). Think about which values you couldn't imagine living without and which ones are less central to your identity and goals.

- *Sample Response: "Here's how I ranked my values: 1. Compassion, 2. Creativity, 3. Adventure, 4. Environmental Stewardship"*

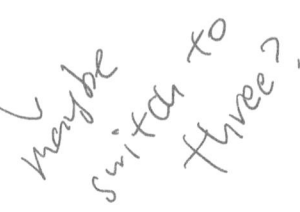
maybe to switch to three?

3. Reflect on Your Top Values: For your top-ranked values (the ones you marked as most important), write a brief reflection on why each of them is significant to you. What do these values represent in your life?

- *Sample Response:* *"Compassion is at the top because I believe in kindness and helping others. Creativity is vital because it allows me to express myself and see the world differently. Adventure represents my thirst for new experiences and growth. Environmental stewardship matters because I want to protect our planet for future generations."*

4. Align Your Life: Lastly, think about how you can align your life with these values. How can you make choices and take actions that honor and reflect your core values?

- *Sample Response:* *"To align my life with these values, I plan to volunteer regularly to support causes that align with compassion. I'll make time for creative pursuits and seek out adventure by exploring new places and trying new activities. I'll also adopt eco-friendly practices in my daily life to support environmental stewardship."*

By completing the Core Values Worksheet, you've taken a significant step in understanding what truly matters to you and how you can live a more authentic and fulfilling life aligned with your values.

Values-Based Decision Making

Now that you've identified your core values, it's time to put them into action. Values-based decision making is all about aligning your choices with the things that matter most to you. This is where the rubber meets the road, and you begin to create a life that truly reflects your values.

Making Choices Aligned with Your Values: Here's how you can make choices that honor your values:

1. Clarify Your Values: Start by reminding yourself of your top values, the ones that truly resonate with you. This will serve as your guiding compass as you navigate decisions in life.

- *Sample Reminder:* *"I remember that my core values are compassion, creativity, adventure, and environmental stewardship."*

2. Evaluate Options: When faced with a decision, consider the options available to you. Think about how each choice aligns with your values. Some choices may align more closely with your values than others.

- *Example Decision:* *"I'm deciding whether to spend my weekend volunteering at an animal shelter or going to a party. Volunteering aligns more with my values of compassion and environmental stewardship."*

3. Prioritize Your Values: Sometimes, you might face choices where multiple values are at play. In such cases, prioritize your values. Which value is more important in this specific situation?

- *Priority Decision:* "In this instance, compassion takes precedence, as I believe in helping others. I can choose to go to the party another time."

4. Reflect on Consequences: Consider the long-term consequences of your choices. Will your decision lead you closer to a values-driven life, or will it take you further away?

- *Consequence Reflection:* "If I volunteer at the animal shelter, I'll be living my values and contributing to a cause I care about. The party might be fun, but it doesn't align with my values as strongly."

5. Take Action: Once you've evaluated your options and reflected on your values, make a conscious choice. Take action in alignment with your core values.

- *Action Step:* "I've decided to volunteer at the animal shelter this weekend. It feels right because it aligns with my values and gives me a sense of fulfillment."

Case Studies Demonstrating the Importance of Commitment to Personal Growth

Let's explore some real-life stories of teenagers who committed to their values and experienced personal growth as a result.

> **Case Study 1: Strengthening Friendships**
>
> *Meet Emma, a teenager who values friendship deeply. She decided to commit to this value by actively nurturing her friendships. Emma started scheduling regular hangouts with her friends, even when she was busy with schoolwork and extracurricular activities. She made an effort to listen actively, provide support, and show appreciation for her friends.*

When Values Are Followed: Emma's commitment to friendship led to stronger bonds with her friends. They felt valued and supported, and their relationships thrived.

When Values Are Not Followed: Before Emma's commitment to friendship, she was often too preoccupied with her own activities and rarely made time for her friends. As a result, her friendships started to feel distant, and some friends even expressed their concerns about her availability.

> **Case Study 2: Building Family Bonds**
>
> *Jake's core value is family, and he wanted to strengthen his connection with his siblings. He committed to spending quality time with them regularly. Jake initiated family game nights, movie nights, and outdoor adventures. By prioritizing these activities, he created lasting memories and deepened his bond with his brothers and sisters.*

When Values Are Followed: Jake's commitment to family brought them closer together. They laughed, played, and supported each other, fostering a strong sense of unity within the family.

When Values Are Not Followed: Before Jake's commitment to family, he often spent time with friends or focused on his personal interests, leaving his siblings feeling neglected and distant. Their relationships were strained, and family gatherings were less enjoyable.

Case Study 3: Excelling in School

Sarah, a teenager passionate about education, made a commitment to excel in school. She set specific academic goals, created a study schedule, and sought help when needed. Sarah consistently attended classes, participated actively, and completed assignments with dedication.

When Values Are Followed: Sarah's commitment to education resulted in improved grades and a deeper understanding of her subjects. She felt a sense of accomplishment and pride in her academic achievements.

When Values Are Not Followed: Prior to Sarah's commitment to education, she often procrastinated and skipped classes. Her grades suffered, and she felt overwhelmed and stressed. Her academic performance did not reflect her true potential.

These case studies highlight the positive impact of committing to personal values and the potential consequences when values are not followed. By aligning actions with values, these teenagers experienced personal growth and improved their relationships and academic performance.

Committing to Values Worksheet

In this worksheet, we will explore the techniques for committing to actions in line with your values. Remember, aligning your choices with your core values is a powerful way to lead a fulfilling and meaningful life.

Step 1: Identify Your Core Values

Before you can commit to your values, it's crucial to know what they are. Refer back to the exercises in the previous sections where you identified your core values.

List your top three core values:

1. _____
2. _____
3. _____

Step 2: Set Value-Based Goals

Values-based goals are specific objectives that align with your core values. They give you a clear direction for how to live in accordance with what truly matters to you.

Write down one value-based goal for each of your top three values:

- *Sample Responses:*

  - *1. Value: Compassion; Goal: Volunteer at the local animal shelter twice a month. "I want to show compassion for animals and help them find loving homes."*

  - *2. Value: Creativity; Goal: Complete one art project each month and share it on social media. "Creativity is essential to me, so I'll express it through my art and connect with others online."*

  - *3. Value: Adventure; Goal: Explore a new hiking trail every other weekend. "Adventure fuels my spirit, and I'll explore nature to satisfy that craving."*

Step 3: Create a Values Vision Board

A values vision board is a visual representation of your core values. It serves as a daily reminder of what you hold dear.

Gather magazines, images, quotes, and symbols that represent each of your core values, and create your own values vision board.

- Use a poster board, corkboard, or a digital platform to assemble your vision board.

- Display it in a place where you can see it daily.

Step 4: Make Value-Based Plans

Once you have set value-based goals, it's time to plan your actions to achieve them.

Choose one value-based goal you've set and outline a plan for achieving it:

- ***Sample Goal:*** *Compassion - Volunteer at the local animal shelter twice a month.*

  - ***Plan:***

    - *Research local animal shelters and contact them to inquire about volunteer opportunities.*

    - *Schedule volunteer shifts on the first and third Saturdays of each month.*

    - *Determine when and how often you will work on this goal: Saturdays from 10 AM to 2 PM.*

Step 5: Accountability Buddy

Share your value-based goals with someone you trust—a friend, family member, or mentor. This person can help keep you accountable and provide support.

Choose someone to be your accountability buddy and share your value-based goals with them:

Accountability Buddy: _____

Step 6: Reflect on Progress

Regularly reflect on your progress toward your value-based goals. Celebrate your successes, and if you face challenges, consider adjustments to stay on track.

- *Sample Response:*

  ○ *Frequency of Review: I'll check in on my goals every Sunday evening to reflect on my progress.*

  ○ *Celebration: Whenever I achieve a goal milestone, I'll treat myself to my favorite dessert as a way to celebrate my achievements.*

Set a schedule for reviewing your progress

How often will you check in on your goals?

What will you do to celebrate your achievements?

Step 7: Revisit and Adjust

Over time, your values and goals may evolve. It's essential to periodically revisit and adjust your goals to align with your changing values.

- *Sample Response:*

  ○ *Frequency of Review: I'll schedule a review of my goals every three months to ensure they still align with my values.*

  ○ *Date of Next Review: My next goal review will be on October 1st.*

Set a reminder to revisit and adjust your value-based goals

Frequency of Review:

Date of Next Review:

Use this worksheet to help you commit to actions that reflect your core values and contribute to your personal growth and well-being. Revisit it regularly to stay on track and make any necessary adjustments as your values and goals evolve.

In Chapter 3, "Thoughts and Feelings," we delved into the intricate relationship between your thoughts and emotions, exploring three vital therapeutic approaches: Cognitive Behavioral Therapy (CBT), Dialectical Behavior Therapy (DBT), and Acceptance and Commitment Therapy (ACT). These approaches have provided you with a toolkit to better understand and manage your inner world.

We started by examining cognitive distortions, those tricky thinking patterns that can lead us astray. You've learned to identify these distortions, challenge them, and replace them with healthier thoughts. This new skill will help you gain control over negative thinking and cultivate a more positive mindset.

Moving on to emotional regulation, we explored the significance of emotions and how they impact your thoughts and behaviors. Equipped with DBT techniques, you now have effective strategies for managing intense emotions, allowing you to navigate life's challenges with resilience.

Lastly, we ventured into the realm of personal values and commitment, a cornerstone of ACT. By identifying your core values through self-reflection, you've gained clarity on what truly matters to you. In the next chapter, you'll learn how to make choices that align with these values, paving the way for a values-driven life.

As you conclude Chapter 3, take pride in the knowledge and skills you've acquired. These insights will serve as a solid foundation as we transition to Chapter 4, "Navigating Challenges." Here, you'll apply what you've learned to tackle real-life obstacles and continue your journey toward personal growth and well-being.

Remember, understanding your thoughts and feelings is a powerful tool, and by embracing these therapeutic techniques, you're taking significant steps toward a happier and more fulfilled life.

4

NAVIGATION CHALLENGES

Introduction

Life can be a rollercoaster ride, right? One moment, you're cruising along smoothly, and the next, you encounter unexpected challenges. That's completely normal. Everyone faces obstacles, big and small, on their journey.

That's where this chapter comes in. It's like your trusty guide through the twists and turns of life's adventure. We're going to delve deeper into these skills and show you how to:

- Fine-tune your problem-solving abilities

- Master the art of embracing tough moments with courage

- Keep your cool when things get tough by expanding on what you've learned

By the end of this chapter, you'll have an even stronger set of skills that will help you navigate life's challenges with confidence and resilience. So, let's dive in and continue to equip you with the tools you need to face whatever comes your way.

Section 1: Problem-Solving with CBT

CBT is like your secret formula for cracking life's code. It equips you with the mindset and techniques to face problems head-on, regardless of whether they're big or small. Here's how CBT can help you conquer life's challenges:

- **Understanding Your Thoughts:** CBT helps you recognize and understand the thoughts and beliefs that might be holding you back. It's like putting on special glasses that help you see through the fog of negative thinking.

- **Managing Your Emotions:** Emotions can sometimes feel like a wild rollercoaster. CBT provides you with the tools to ride that rollercoaster with control. Think of it as having an emotional seatbelt.

- **Changing Unhelpful Patterns:** Have you ever felt stuck in a loop of unhelpful behaviors? CBT helps you identify those patterns and break free from them. It's like having a personal escape plan.

- **Setting Achievable Goals:** CBT helps you set realistic and achievable goals, whether it's acing a test, improving relationships, or managing stress. It's like having a treasure map to your dreams.

Identifying Problems (CBT)

Alright, let's roll up our sleeves and start our problem-solving journey by becoming pros at identifying the issues that are bugging us.

Why it matters:

Identifying problems is like shining a spotlight on what needs fixing. You can't solve what you can't see! It's like spotting a hidden treasure; you need a map first.

- **Example 1: School - Homework Overload**

You're drowning in a sea of homework assignments, and you're stressed because you also want some free time. What's the problem here? Identifying the problem means realizing that it's about finding a balance between schoolwork and leisure.

- **Example 2: Family - Sibling Conflict**

You and your younger sibling are constantly bickering over the TV remote. It's causing chaos at home, and your parents have asked you to find a solution. What's the problem? Identifying it means recognizing that it's about resolving conflicts and sharing responsibilities fairly.

- **Example 3: School - Peer Pressure**

Your school buddies are pressuring you to skip class and join them in something you know is wrong. You want to maintain your grades and avoid trouble. What's the problem here? Identifying it means understanding that it's about making choices that align with your values while navigating peer pressure.

- **Example 4: Family - Chores and Responsibilities**

Your parents want you to step up with more chores, like doing the dishes and cleaning your room. Balancing this with school and hobbies is tough. What's the problem? Identifying it means realizing that it's about managing responsibilities effectively.

- **Example 5: Friends - Misunderstanding**

You had a falling-out with one of your close friends, causing tension in your group. You want to mend the friendship and clear the air. What's the problem? Identifying it means acknowledging that it's about resolving conflicts and rebuilding trust within your friendship circle.

How to do it:

Identifying problems is all about recognizing what's bothering you or causing challenges in your life. By pinpointing the problems, you're taking the first crucial step toward finding solutions and making positive changes.

Now that we've got a handle on identifying problems, let's move on to the exciting part—generating solutions!

Generating Solutions (CBT)

Generating solutions is like having a treasure chest full of options to choose from. The more solutions you have, the better chance you'll find the perfect one. It's like having a toolbox with various tools for different tasks.

How to do it:

Okay, let's break it down into steps:

1. **Brainstorm:** This is your time to let your imagination run wild. Think of as many potential solutions as

you can, even if they seem a bit out there. There are no bad ideas in brainstorming.

2. **Get Creative:** Think outside the box! Consider unconventional approaches or ideas you haven't tried before. Creativity is your secret weapon.

3. **Ask for Input:** Don't be afraid to ask friends, family, or mentors for their input. They might have some brilliant ideas you haven't thought of.

4. **Use Past Successes:** Reflect on times when you've overcome similar challenges in the past. What worked then? Could those strategies apply now?

5. **Consider Pros and Cons:** As you brainstorm, think about the potential pros and cons of each solution. It's like evaluating the strengths and weaknesses of different game strategies.

Now, let's apply these steps to each of our sample scenarios:

1. School - Homework Overload:

- Brainstorm solutions:

  ◦ Creating a study schedule to manage your time better.

  ◦ Asking a teacher for help with challenging assignments.

  ◦ Forming a study group with classmates to share the workload.

  ◦ Using educational apps or online resources for extra support.

2. Family - Sibling Conflict:

- Brainstorm solutions:

  ◦ Setting a schedule for TV time to avoid conflicts.

  ◦ Creating a rotation system for using the TV remote.

  ◦ Discussing and agreeing on shows or programs to watch together.

  ◦ Designating specific remote times for each family member.

3. School - Peer Pressure:

- Brainstorm solutions:

[handwritten note in right margin: I changed my opinion. I think even the long examples should be italicized]

- ◦ Politely declining invitations without giving in to pressure.

- ◦ Finding alternative activities to suggest to your friends.

- ◦ Talking to a trusted adult or school counselor about the peer pressure.

- ◦ Making new friends who share your values and interests.

4. Family - Chores and Responsibilities:

- Brainstorm solutions:

  - ◦ Creating a chore chart with specific tasks and responsibilities.

  - ◦ Setting a daily or weekly schedule for completing chores.

  - ◦ Negotiating with your parents for a fair division of chores.

  - ◦ Using incentives or rewards for completing chores efficiently.

5. Friends - Misunderstanding:

- Brainstorm solutions:

  - ◦ Initiating an open and honest conversation with your friend to clear up the misunderstanding.

  - ◦ Asking a mutual friend to help mediate the conversation.

  - ◦ Writing a heartfelt letter or message to express your feelings and intentions.

  - ◦ Organizing a fun group activity to reconnect and rebuild trust.

Exploring Additional Options: Considerations for Each Problem

Sometimes, when facing various challenges in life, it's important to acknowledge that multiple solutions might cross our minds – some of which may not be the best course of action. In this section, we'll take a closer look at these alternative options, keeping in mind that we will later examine their pros and cons to determine their suitability.

1. School - Homework Overload:

- Not doing the homework and hoping the teacher won't notice.

- Complaining to the teacher about the workload without proposing solutions.

- Procrastinating until the last minute and rushing through assignments.

- Copying homework from classmates as a regular practice.

2. Family - Sibling Conflict:

- Hiding or taking the TV remote to prevent others from using it.

- Ignoring the conflict and avoiding family members altogether.

- Resorting to physical confrontation over the remote.

- Blaming one family member for all the conflicts and not taking responsibility.

3. School - Peer Pressure:

- Giving in to peer pressure to fit in and please friends.

- Isolating yourself completely to avoid any peer pressure situations.

- Spreading rumors or gossip to divert attention from yourself.

- Using substances like alcohol or drugs to cope with peer pressure.

4. Family - Chores and Responsibilities:

- Refusing to do any chores altogether.

- Constantly arguing with your parents about chores without seeking a resolution.

- Doing chores poorly on purpose to avoid being assigned more tasks.

- Using bribery or manipulation to get out of chores.

5. Friends - Misunderstanding:

- Holding a grudge and not addressing the misunderstanding.

- Talking negatively about your friend behind their back.

- Using passive-aggressive behavior to express your feelings.

- Cutting off all communication with your friend without explanation.

While these alternatives may come to mind, it's important to remember that they require careful consideration of their pros and cons before deciding on a course of action that is both constructive and respectful of yourself and others.

Remember, these are just a starting point. The more solutions you brainstorm, the better equipped you'll be to choose the one that feels right for your unique situation. So, let's get those creative gears turning and come up with some fantastic ideas!

Evaluating Solutions (CBT)

Now that we've brainstormed a bunch of solutions, it's time to put on our detective hats and figure out which ones are the best fit for our challenges.

How to do it:

Let's break it down:

1. Pros and Cons List: Make a list of the potential advantages (pros) and disadvantages (cons) for each solution. This is like making a balance sheet for your ideas.

2. Realistic Expectations: Think about how feasible and realistic each solution is. Are you capable of carrying it out, given your resources and circumstances? It's like choosing a path that's doable.

3. Impact Assessment: Consider how each solution might affect you and those around you. Will it make things better, worse, or stay the same? It's like predicting the outcome of your choices.

4. Prioritization: Decide which solutions align best with your values and goals. Some solutions might be more important or urgent than others. It's like sorting through your options based on what matters most.

1. School - Homework Overload:

Pros and Cons List:

- Creating a study schedule (Pros: better time management, Cons: need to stick to the schedule).

- Asking a teacher for help (Pros: understanding difficult topics, Cons: may require extra time).

- Forming a study group (Pros: shared workload, Cons: coordinating schedules).

- Using educational apps (Pros: accessible resources, Cons: screen time management).

- Not doing homework (Pros: immediate relief, Cons: academic consequences).

- Copying homework (Pros: quick fix, Cons: unethical and risky).

- Procrastinating (Pros: temporary stress relief, Cons: high-pressure situation).

2. Family - Sibling Conflict:

Pros and Cons List:

- Setting a schedule for TV time (Pros: structured, Cons: requires adherence).

- Creating a rotation system for the remote (Pros: fairness, Cons: may cause disputes).

- Discussing and agreeing on shows (Pros: shared decision, Cons: may lead to disagreements).

- Designating specific remote times (Pros: clear allocation, Cons: rigid schedule).

- Hiding the TV remote (Pros: immediate control, Cons: fosters secrecy and conflicts).

- Ignoring conflicts (Pros: avoidance, Cons: unresolved issues).

- Resorting to physical confrontation (Pros: temporary dominance, Cons: escalates conflicts).

- Blaming one family member (Pros: deflecting responsibility, Cons: unfair and unproductive).

3. School - Peer Pressure:

Pros and Cons List:

- Politely declining invitations (Pros: assertiveness, Cons: potential conflict).

- Finding alternative activities (Pros: positive choices, Cons: might miss out on some fun).

- Talking to a trusted adult (Pros: guidance, Cons: may feel uncomfortable).

- Making new friends (Pros: shared values, Cons: change can be challenging).

- Giving in to peer pressure (Pros: short-term acceptance, Cons: compromising personal values).

- Isolating yourself (Pros: avoidance, Cons: loneliness and isolation).

- Spreading rumors (Pros: diversion, Cons: harmful and unethical).

- Using substances (Pros: momentary relief, Cons: health and legal risks).

4. Family - Chores and Responsibilities:

Pros and Cons List:

- Creating a chore chart (Pros: clear tasks, Cons: need to follow the chart).

- Setting a schedule (Pros: routine, Cons: may require adjustments).

- Negotiating with parents (Pros: mutual agreement, Cons: may need compromise).

- Using incentives or rewards (Pros: motivation, Cons: may not always work).

- Refusing to do chores (Pros: immediate avoidance, Cons: strain on family dynamics).

- Constantly arguing (Pros: expressing frustration, Cons: stressful environment).

- Doing chores poorly (Pros: avoidance, Cons: increased workload for others).

- Using bribery or manipulation (Pros: short-term relief, Cons: erodes trust).

5. Friends - Misunderstanding:

Pros and Cons List:

- Open and honest conversation (Pros: clarity, Cons: vulnerability).

- Mediation by a mutual friend (Pros: neutral party, Cons: may not resolve underlying issues).

- Writing a heartfelt message (Pros: thoughtful, Cons: may not convey tone well).

- Organizing a group activity (Pros: shared experience, Cons: may require planning).

- Holding a grudge (Pros: temporary emotional distance, Cons: long-term strain on friendship).

- Talking negatively (Pros: venting, Cons: damage to reputation).

- Using passive-aggressive behavior (Pros: expression of frustration, Cons: escalates tension).

- Cutting off communication (Pros: avoidance, Cons: may result in permanent estrangement).

Remember, the evaluation process helps you choose the solution that best fits your unique situation and goals. It's like selecting the perfect tool from your toolbox for the job at hand. Now, let's continue refining our problem-solving skills by making a plan!

Making a Plan (CBT)

Now that we've evaluated our solutions, it's time to roll up our sleeves and create action plans to tackle those challenges head-on.

Making a plan is like drawing a roadmap to reach your destination. It helps you stay on track and focused on your goals. Think of it as your treasure map to success!

How to do it:

Let's break down the process into actionable steps:

1. Set Clear Goals: Define what you want to achieve with this plan.

2. Break it Down: Divide your plan into smaller, manageable steps. This makes big tasks feel less overwhelming. It's like breaking a challenging game level into smaller quests.

3. Set Deadlines: Assign deadlines to each step. This keeps you accountable and ensures you're making progress. It's like having a countdown timer for your tasks.

4. Allocate Resources: Determine what you need to execute your plan. It could be time, tools, support from others, or specific skills. Think of it as gathering the right equipment for your quest.

5. Track Progress: Regularly check your progress against your plan. Adjust as needed if things aren't going as expected. It's like using a map and adjusting your route if you encounter detours.

Now, let's apply these steps to our sample scenarios:

1. School - Homework Overload:

Goal: Manage homework and free time effectively.

Steps:

    1. Create a study schedule with dedicated time for each subject.

    2. Identify challenging topics and seek help from teachers or classmates.

    3. Form a study group and agree on study sessions.

    4. Explore educational apps and incorporate them into your study routine.

    • Deadlines: Set a weekly schedule.

- Resources: Study materials, a quiet place to study, and support from teachers and friends.

2. Family - Sibling Conflict:

Goal: Resolve conflicts over the TV remote and maintain peace at home.

Steps:

1. Discuss with your sibling and agree on a schedule for TV time.

2. Create a rotation system for using the remote fairly.

3. Choose and plan TV shows or programs to watch together.

4. Stick to the agreed-upon schedule.

- Deadlines: Start the schedule immediately.

- Resources: A shared calendar, a list of preferred shows, and family cooperation.

3. School - Peer Pressure:

Goal: Make choices aligned with personal values while maintaining friendships.

Steps:

1. Politely decline invitations with confidence.

2. Seek alternative activities that align with your values.

3. Engage in open communication with your friends about your choices.

4. Explore new friendships with like-minded peers.

- Deadlines: Ongoing.

- Resources: Communication skills, alternative activity ideas, and support from trusted adults.

4. Family - Chores and Responsibilities:

Goal: Manage responsibilities effectively while balancing school and activities.

Steps:

1. Create a chore chart with assigned tasks and schedules.

2. Set a daily routine for completing chores.

3. Discuss and negotiate with parents for fair division of responsibilities.

4. Establish a reward system for completing chores.

- Deadlines: Start the chore chart and routine immediately.

- Resources: Chore list, a daily schedule, negotiation skills, and incentives.

5. Friends - Misunderstanding:

Goal: Resolve the misunderstanding and rebuild trust within your friendship group.

Steps:

1. Initiate an open and honest conversation with your friend to clear up the misunderstanding.

2. Consider involving a mutual friend to mediate the conversation if needed.

3. Write a heartfelt message expressing your feelings and intentions.

4. Organize a fun group activity to reconnect and strengthen bonds.

- Deadlines: Plan and initiate the conversation soon.

- Resources: Effective communication skills, support from friends, and creative activity ideas.

With these action plans in place, you're equipped with clear steps to take on your challenges and work toward positive solutions. Remember, just like in a video game, you've got your quest objectives laid out. Now, let's go out there and conquer those challenges!

Real-World Problem-Solving Worksheet

Problem-solving is a valuable skill that can help you navigate challenges in various areas of your life, including school, family, and friendships. This worksheet will guide you through real-life scenarios and activities to practice problem-solving techniques.

Real-Life Scenario 1: School - Homework Overload

Scenario: You've created a study schedule, but you're struggling to stick to it consistently. What do you do?

Activity:

1. Track Your Study Habits: Record your study habits for a week, noting when and where you study, and any distractions or difficulties you encounter.

> **My Study Habits:**
> - Study Time:
> - Study Location:
> - Distractions:

2. Identify Obstacles: Based on your tracking, identify obstacles that make it challenging to follow your schedule.

> - Obstacle 1:
> - Obstacle 2:
> - Obstacle 3:

3. Brainstorm Solutions: Think of creative solutions to overcome these obstacles and adjust your study schedule accordingly.

- Solution 1:

- Solution 2:

- Solution 3:

4. Implement Changes: Put your new schedule into action and track your progress.

Progress:
Day 1:
Day 2:
Day 3:

Here's a sample response for each prompt in the scenario of dealing with a study schedule and struggling to stick to it consistently:

My Study Habits:

- Study Time: 8:00 PM - 10:00 PM

- Study Location: My bedroom

- Distractions: Phone notifications, noisy neighbors, snacks

Obstacles:

- Obstacle 1: Phone notifications keep diverting my attention.

- Obstacle 2: Noisy neighbors create a disruptive environment.

- Obstacle 3: Frequent snacking leads to unnecessary breaks.

italicize ?

Solutions:

- Solution 1: Put my phone on silent or in another room while studying to minimize distractions.

- Solution 2: Use noise-canceling headphones or move to a quieter space, like the library, during study hours.

- Solution 3: Prepare healthy snacks in advance and limit access to tempting, distracting foods during study time.

Progress:

- Day 1: Implemented Solution 1, was able to study with fewer interruptions.

- Day 2: Applied Solution 2, enjoyed a more peaceful study environment.

- Day 3: Implemented Solution 3, had healthier snacks on hand and reduced breaks.

Real-Life Scenario 2: Family - Sibling Conflict

Scenario: Your sibling broke the TV remote by accident. It's your turn to use it, but it's not working. What's your next move?

Activity:

1. Assess the Situation: Take a deep breath and assess the situation calmly.

Assessment:
- What happened?
- How do you feel?

2. Consider Options: Think of possible solutions, such as fixing the remote, getting a replacement, or finding alternative entertainment.

- Option 1:
- Option 2:
- Option 3:

3. Discuss with Sibling and Parents: Have a conversation with your sibling and involve your parents if necessary to find a resolution.

Discussion Notes:
- Sibling's Perspective:
- Parent's Input:

4. Agree on a Solution: Collaborate with your sibling and parents to choose the best solution.

> • **Agreed Solution:**

Here's a sample response for each prompt in the scenario of a sibling breaking the TV remote:

Assessment:

- What happened? My sibling accidentally broke the TV remote.

- How do you feel? I feel frustrated because it's my turn to use the remote, and it's not working due to the accident.

Options:

- Option 1: Try to fix the remote by checking if the batteries are properly inserted or if there's visible damage that can be repaired.

- Option 2: If the remote can't be fixed, ask my parents if they have a spare remote or if they can help replace it.

- Option 3: Find an alternative form of entertainment that doesn't require the TV, like playing a board game or going outside for some fresh air.

Discussion Notes:

- Sibling's Perspective: My sibling admits it was an accident and feels sorry about it. They didn't mean to break the remote.

- Parent's Input: My parents suggest checking if we have a spare remote or if we can temporarily use a universal remote until we can replace the broken one.

Agreed Solution: We agree to use a universal remote temporarily, and we'll look into getting a replacement for the broken remote. This way, we can still enjoy TV without any conflicts.

Real-Life Scenario 3: School - Peer Pressure

Scenario: Your friends are pressuring you to skip school to hang out with them. You want to maintain your attendance but also keep your friendships intact. What's your plan?

Activity:

1. Assertive Communication: Politely decline their invitation and suggest an alternative plan, such as meeting up after school or on the weekend.

> **My Response:**

2. Stay Committed: Stick to your school attendance goal while making an effort to maintain your friendships in ways that align with your values.

> **Commitment:**

Here's a sample response for each prompt in the scenario of dealing with peer pressure to skip school:

My Response:

"Hey, thanks for the invite to chill today! You know I love hanging with you guys, and our friendship means a ton to me. But honestly, I'm all about keeping up my school attendance right now because it's a big deal for my education and future goals. How 'bout we plan to meet up after school or on the weekend? We can still have a blast and catch up without me missing out on school stuff."

Commitment:

I'm committed to prioritizing my school attendance while also nurturing my friendships in a way that aligns with my values and goals. This means I will continue to make the effort to stay connected with my friends and find alternative times to hang out that don't interfere with my school commitments. It's important to me to strike a balance between my education and maintaining meaningful relationships with my friends.

Real-Life Scenario 4: Family - Chores and Responsibilities

Scenario: You and your sibling have an argument about who should do the dishes tonight. How can you resolve this quickly?

Activity:

1. Negotiation: Use negotiation skills to discuss the situation with your sibling.

> **Negotiation Notes:**
> - Your Proposal:
>
> - Sibling's Proposal:

2. Consider Compromises: Explore compromises, such as taking turns doing the dishes or agreeing on a schedule.

> - **Compromise Agreement:**

3. Create a Fair System: Collaborate with your sibling to create a fair system that both of you can follow.

> - **Fair System:**

Here's a sample response for each prompt in the scenario of an argument with your sibling about doing the dishes:

Negotiation Notes:

- *Your Proposal: "How about we take turns doing the dishes? I'll do them tonight, and you can do them tomorrow. That way, it's fair and neither of us has to do them every night."*

- *Sibling's Proposal: "I think it's better if we create a schedule for the week. We can each have specific days when we're responsible for the dishes, so it's predictable."*

Compromise Agreement:

After discussing, we agree to go with the schedule idea proposed by my sibling. We create a fair schedule where we both have set days for doing the dishes throughout the week, making it more organized and predictable.

Fair System:

- *Monday: You do the dishes.*

- *Tuesday: Sibling does the dishes.*

- *Wednesday: You do the dishes.*

- *Thursday: Sibling does the dishes.*

- *Friday: You do the dishes.*

- *Saturday: Sibling does the dishes.*

- *Sunday: You do the dishes.*

This system ensures that both of us have an equal share of responsibility, and there's no need for frequent arguments over who should do the dishes each night.

Real-Life Scenario 5: Friends - Misunderstanding

Scenario: You've had an open and honest conversation with your friend to clear up the misunderstanding. However, tensions are still high. How can you rebuild trust?

Activity:

1. Plan a Group Activity: Organize a fun and inclusive group activity with your friends, such as a movie night or a game day.

Activity Plan:
- Activity:

- Date and Time:

- Invite Friends:

2. Create Positive Experiences: Focus on creating positive shared experiences with your friends to rebuild trust over time.

> • **Positive Experiences:**

Here's a sample response for each prompt in the scenario of trying to rebuild trust with friends after a misunderstanding:

Activity Plan:

- *Activity: Let's plan a relaxed movie night at my place.*

- *Date and Time: Friday evening at 7:00 PM.*

- *Invite Friends: I'll invite the friends who were involved in the misunderstanding, plus a few more close friends to keep it inclusive.*

Positive Experiences:

- *During the movie night, we all had a great time laughing and enjoying each other's company.*

- *We shared some snacks, discussed the movie, and even played some fun games afterward.*

- *It was a positive and relaxed atmosphere that helped dissipate tension and rebuild trust among us.*

- *We plan to continue organizing similar group activities to strengthen our friendships and move past the misunderstanding.*

Conclusion

Problem-solving is a dynamic skill that improves with practice. By tackling real-world scenarios and applying problem-solving techniques, you can become a more effective and confident problem solver in various aspects of your life.

Section 2: Acceptance Strategies with ACT

Welcome to Section 2, where we will delve into the powerful world of Acceptance Strategies within the framework of Acceptance and Commitment Therapy (ACT). In this section, we'll explore how embracing acceptance and fostering psychological flexibility can significantly enhance your ability to manage life's challenges effectively.

Now, let's commence our exploration of the first facet of ACT: Acceptance vs. Avoidance.

Acceptance vs. Avoidance

In the world of Acceptance and Commitment Therapy (ACT), one of the foundational concepts revolves around the choice between acceptance and avoidance when faced with difficult thoughts, feelings, or situations. Understanding this fundamental distinction can profoundly impact how you navigate life's challenges.

Acceptance:

- Acceptance involves acknowledging and embracing your thoughts, emotions, and experiences without judgment or resistance.

- It's like saying, "I acknowledge that this is how I feel, and it's okay." This doesn't mean you have to like or agree with what's happening, but it's about allowing it to be present.

- Acceptance allows you to be in tune with your inner experiences and opens the door to understanding and growth.

Avoidance:

- Avoidance, on the other hand, refers to the attempts to escape, suppress, or ignore uncomfortable thoughts, emotions, or situations.

- It's akin to saying, "I don't want to feel this way, so I'll do whatever it takes to avoid it." While avoidance may offer temporary relief, it often leads to increased distress in the long run.

- Avoidance can manifest as distractions, substance use, or avoiding challenging conversations and situations.

Why Acceptance Matters:

Acceptance is a cornerstone of emotional resilience and psychological flexibility. It empowers you to confront life's difficulties with courage and wisdom.

By choosing acceptance, you create space for understanding and transformation. You can learn from your experiences and make choices aligned with your values.

Sample Scenarios

1. School Performance - Exam Anxiety:

- **Acceptance:** *Acknowledging and allowing the feelings of anxiety about an upcoming exam without trying to suppress or avoid them.*

- **Avoidance:** *Trying to distract yourself from anxiety by procrastinating or avoiding studying altogether.*

2. Family Conflict - Heated Argument:

- **Acceptance:** *Recognizing and accepting the anger and frustration you feel during a heated family argument without denying or suppressing these emotions.*

- **Avoidance:** *Attempting to escape the argument by leaving the room or refusing to engage in the discussion.*

3. Friendship - Disagreement with a Friend:

- **Acceptance:** *Accepting that you and your friend have differing opinions or values in a respectful and non-judgmental way.*

- **Avoidance**: *Avoiding addressing the disagreement and pretending it doesn't exist to maintain a superficial harmony in the friendship.*

These sample scenarios illustrate the choices between acceptance and avoidance that you might encounter in various aspects of your life. As we delve deeper into this section, you'll gain a better understanding of how to navigate these choices effectively.

Exercises in Acceptance

Exercise 1: Weathering the Storm

Objective: Practice accepting difficult emotions without judgment.

1. Choose an Emotion: Identify a challenging emotion you've been experiencing lately, like anger, sadness, or anxiety.

2. Mindful Observation: Find a quiet space, close your eyes, and take a few deep breaths. Allow the chosen emotion to arise without resisting it.

3. Observe Sensations: Pay attention to the physical sensations associated with this emotion. Where do you feel it in your body? Is there tension, heat, or discomfort?

4. Naming Without Judgment: Name the emotion in your mind without judgment. For example, say, "I am feeling anger right now," or "I am experiencing sadness."

5. Refrain from Analysis: Resist the urge to analyze or justify the emotion. Accept it as a valid part of your experience.

6. Breathe Through It: Take slow, deep breaths as you continue to observe the emotion. Imagine your breath flowing in and out of the area where you feel it in your body.

7. Release and Let Go: After a few minutes, open your eyes and let go of the focus on the emotion. Acknowledge that it's okay to feel this way, and you can choose how to respond to it.

Exercise 2: The Sound of Silence

Objective: Practice accepting moments of silence without filling them with distractions.

1. Set a Timer: Choose a specific time, like 10 minutes, to dedicate to this exercise.

2. Create Silence: Find a comfortable, quiet space with no external distractions. Turn off your devices and put them out of reach.

3. Sit in Silence: Sit comfortably and close your eyes. Allow yourself to sit in complete silence for the duration you've chosen.

4. Observation: As you sit in silence, observe any thoughts, feelings, or impulses to fill the silence with noise or distractions.

5. Accept the Silence: Instead of filling the silence, accept it as it is. Embrace the stillness and allow your mind to wander or rest without judgment.

6. Return to the Present: If your mind starts to wander into thoughts, gently bring your focus back to the present moment and the silence around you.

7. Reflect: After the exercise, reflect on your experience. Did you notice any discomfort or resistance to the silence? What did you learn from embracing it?

Exercise 3: Radical Self-Compassion

Objective: Practice self-compassion by accepting and embracing your imperfections.

1. Choose a Self-Criticism: Identify a common self-criticism or negative self-talk that you often engage in.

2. Reframe with Compassion: Whenever this self-criticism arises, reframe it with a compassionate statement. For example, if you often criticize yourself for making mistakes, say, "It's okay to make mistakes; I am learning and growing."

3. Write It Down: Keep a journal of these self-compassionate reframes whenever you notice self-criticism.

4. Reflect: Periodically review your journal entries and reflect on how practicing self-compassion has affected your self-esteem and emotional well-being.

These exercises will help you practice acceptance in various aspects of your life, promoting emotional well-being and self-compassion. Remember that acceptance is an ongoing practice, and it's okay to revisit these exercises regularly.

The Concept of Psychological Flexibility vs. Inflexibility

The concept of psychological flexibility shines as a guiding light towards resilience and personal growth. It's not just a concept; it's a profound philosophy that can reshape how you engage with your inner world and the world around you.

Understanding Psychological Flexibility:

- Psychological flexibility is the ability to adapt and respond to life's challenges with an open and accepting mindset.

- It's like being a willow tree, bending gracefully with the winds of change rather than standing rigid and brittle.

- Psychological flexibility involves staying open to your thoughts and emotions, even when they are uncomfortable, and taking actions aligned with your values despite the discomfort.

Key Components of Psychological Flexibility:

1. Acceptance: Acknowledging and making space for all your thoughts and emotions, whether they are pleasant or distressing.

2. Present Moment Awareness: Engaging fully in the present moment without judgment, instead of dwelling on the past or worrying about the future.

3. Defusion: Creating distance from your thoughts by recognizing that they are just thoughts, not absolute facts.

4. Values Clarification: Identifying and clarifying your core values, the things that genuinely matter to you.

5. Committed Action: Taking purposeful steps and actions that align with your values, even in the face of discomfort.

The Consequences of Psychological Inflexibility:

On the flip side, psychological inflexibility involves resisting, avoiding, or denying your thoughts, emotions, or challenging situations.

It's like trying to build a house on shifting sands; it leads to instability and distress.

Psychological inflexibility often results in increased emotional suffering, strained relationships, and an inability to live a meaningful life.

Sample Scenarios Illustrating Psychological Flexibility vs. Inflexibility

1. School Performance - Imperfect Presentation:

- **Psychological Flexibility:** *Embracing the nervousness and imperfection of your presentation, staying present during the speech, and delivering it in alignment with your commitment to personal growth.*

- **Psychological Inflexibility:** *Denying nervousness, attempting to suppress it, and delivering the presentation with increased anxiety, leading to a less effective performance.*

2. Family Conflict - Differences of Opinion:

- **Psychological Flexibility:** *Engaging in a family discussion with an open mind, accepting that different opinions exist, and focusing on maintaining a loving and respectful connection despite differences.*

- **Psychological Inflexibility:** *Resisting differing opinions, becoming defensive, and escalating the conflict, leading to strained family relationships.*

3. Friendship - Handling a Misunderstanding:

- **Psychological Flexibility:** *Acknowledging the discomfort of a misunderstanding with a friend, defusing from negative thoughts, and taking actions to clarify the situation while staying true to your core values.*

- **Psychological Inflexibility:** *Avoiding addressing the misunderstanding, letting negative thoughts fester, and potentially damaging the friendship further due to lack of communication.*

Understanding the contrast between psychological flexibility and inflexibility highlights the profound impact these mindsets can have on your well-being and the quality of your relationships. As we delve deeper into the realm of psychological flexibility, you'll discover how this concept can transform the way you navigate the complexities of life.

Defusion Techniques

Defusion techniques play a vital role in helping you distance yourself from your thoughts and break free from their overwhelming influence. Think of these techniques as your toolkit for untangling from the web of negative or distressing thoughts.

What is Defusion?

Defusion is the process of creating space between yourself and your thoughts. It's about recognizing that thoughts are just words and mental events, not concrete realities.

Imagine thoughts as passing clouds in the sky; they come and go, but they don't define your existence.

Defusion techniques help you unhook from the grip of thoughts, allowing you to observe them with a sense of detachment.

Key Defusion Techniques

1. Name and Observe: Give your thoughts funny or quirky names. For example, if you have a self-doubting thought, you might call it "The Self-Doubt DJ." This playful approach can help you detach from the thought's seriousness.

2. Sing It: Sing your troubling thoughts to a familiar tune, making them sound absurd. It's hard to take a thought seriously when it's sung to the tune of a catchy song.

3. Thank Your Mind: When a distressing thought arises, thank your mind for sharing it, as if it's a well-intentioned friend. This shifts your perspective and reduces the thought's impact.

4. Object Observation: Describe an object in detail, focusing on its color, shape, texture, and other sensory details. This anchors you in the present moment and diverts attention from troubling thoughts.

5. Mindful Breathing: Pay close attention to your breath, observing its rhythm and sensations. This mindfulness practice helps you stay centered and reduces thought interference.

Why Defusion Matters

Defusion liberates you from the grip of unhelpful or distressing thoughts, fostering emotional well-being and mental clarity.

It allows you to respond to thoughts with choice and intention, rather than reacting impulsively.

Sample Scenarios Illustrating Defusion Techniques

1. Performance Anxiety - Upcoming Presentation:

- **Defusion Technique:** Naming self-doubting thoughts as "The Stage Fright Monster" and observing them with curiosity rather than fear.

2. Relationship Stress - Worries About a Friend's Reaction:

- **Defusion Technique:** Singing anxious thoughts about your friend's reaction to a humorous tune, making them seem less daunting.

3. Academic Pressure - Fear of Failure:

- **Defusion Technique:** Thanking your mind for sharing thoughts about failure and seeing them as well-intentioned warnings rather than inevitable outcomes.

As you explore and practice these defusion techniques, you'll gain a valuable skill set for navigating the sometimes turbulent waters of your inner world with greater ease and resilience.

Defusion Techniques Worksheet

Introduction

This worksheet will guide you through five key defusion techniques, each designed to help you detach from distressing thoughts and gain greater control over your inner world.

Technique 1: Name and Observe

1. Name the Thought: Identify a distressing or unhelpful thought that you often encounter.

2. Give It a Playful Name: Come up with a fun, quirky name for the thought. Be creative and make it lighthearted.

3. Observe with Detachment: When the thought arises, remind yourself of its playful name and observe it with curiosity. How does this change your relationship with the thought?

I liked the other boxes from the other worksheets

Technique 2: Sing It

1. Choose a Familiar Tune: Select a catchy song or tune that you're familiar with.

2. Sing the Thought: When a distressing thought emerges, sing it to the chosen tune. You can make up your own lyrics or use the thought's content.

3. Observe Your Reaction: Notice how singing the thought affects your perception of it. Does it make the thought seem less serious or overwhelming?

Technique 3: Thank Your Mind

1. Acknowledge a Distressing Thought: Identify a thought that often triggers anxiety or discomfort.

2. Express Gratitude: When this thought arises, thank your mind for sharing it with you. Imagine it as a well-intentioned friend trying to protect you.

3. Reflect on Your Feelings: How does expressing gratitude toward the thought change the way you feel about it? Does it reduce its impact?

Technique 4: Object Observation

1. Select an Object: Find an object in your environment, such as a pen, a book, or a cup.

2. Detailed Observation: Focus your attention on the object's sensory details. Describe its color, shape, texture, and any other characteristics.

3. Shift Your Focus: When a distressing thought arises, shift your attention to the object and engage in detailed observation. How does this practice affect your relationship with the thought?

Conclusion

As you explore and practice these defusion techniques, you'll develop a valuable skill set for managing distressing or unhelpful thoughts. Remember that these techniques are tools to help you gain greater control over your inner world, fostering emotional well-being and mental clarity.

Being Present vs. The Consequences of Not Being Present

The concept of "being present" stands as a cornerstone of mindfulness and emotional well-being. Being present means fully engaging in the current moment, without judgment or distraction, and it's a practice that can profoundly transform your relationship with your inner experiences.

What Does "Being Present" Mean?

- Being present involves immersing yourself in the here and now, paying full attention to the present moment.

- It's akin to becoming an active participant in your own life story, rather than a passive observer.

- Being present means experiencing life's sights, sounds, and sensations with a sense of curiosity and openness.

Key Practices for Being Present:

1. Mindful Breathing: Focus on your breath, observing its natural rhythm and the sensations it brings.

2. Sensory Awareness: Engage your senses in the present moment. Notice the details of what you see, hear, touch, taste, and smell.

3. Non-Judgmental Observation: When thoughts or emotions arise, observe them without labeling them as "good" or "bad." They are simply passing mental events.

4. Grounding Exercises: Use techniques like grounding to anchor yourself in the present. For example, notice the sensation of your feet on the ground or the weight of an object in your hand.

The Consequences of Not Being Present:

- When you're not present, life can feel like a blur, as if you're sleepwalking through your own existence.

- You might find it challenging to fully engage with your experiences, leading to a sense of detachment and emptiness.

- Emotions can become overwhelming when you're not present, as they catch you off guard, leaving you feeling reactive and out of control.

- Relationships may suffer when you're not fully present with loved ones, leading to misunderstandings and disconnection.

Sample Scenarios Illustrating Being Present:

1. Nature Walk - Sensory Immersion:

- **Being Present Practice:** During a walk in nature, immerse yourself in the sensory experience. Notice the rustling leaves, the chirping of birds, and the feel of the earth beneath your feet.

2. Mealtime - Mindful Eating:

- **Being Present Practice:** During a meal, focus on the taste, texture, and aroma of each bite. Eat slowly and savor each mouthful.

3. Stressful Meeting - Non-Judgmental Observation:

- **Being Present Practice:** In a stressful work meeting, observe your thoughts and emotions without judgment. Recognize them as passing mental events and bring your attention back to the discussion.

By practicing being present, you can bring a greater sense of clarity and mindfulness to your daily life. This practice enables you to fully engage with your experiences and respond to them with intention and authenticity.

Section 3: Thriving Through Life's Storms with Distress Tolerance

Welcome to the third section of our journey, where we explore the invaluable skill of Distress Tolerance. Just as sailors prepare for rough seas, we too need tools to navigate life's storms without losing our way. This section serves as your compass to understanding and mastering Distress Tolerance, a vital component of Dialectical Behavior Therapy (DBT).

In the pages that follow, we'll equip you with essential Distress Tolerance skills to confront life's challenges head-on.

Skill Set 1: Crisis Survival Skills

Crisis Survival Skills are particularly useful when emotions run high, and it feels like you're in the middle of a crisis.

Purpose: Techniques for coping with overwhelming emotions and crisis situations.

- In moments of crisis, it's common to feel like you're drowning in a sea of emotions. Crisis Survival Skills are designed to provide you with effective techniques to keep your head above water and regain a sense of control.

A. Review of TIPP Skills (Temperature, Intense Exercise, Paced Breathing): Techniques to quickly reduce emotional intensity.

- **Temperature:**

  - **Technique:** Use cold water or ice packs on your face or immerse your hands in cold water for 30 seconds.

  - **How It Helps:** The shock of cold temperature can quickly shift your focus away from distressing emotions and provide a moment of relief.

- **Intense Exercise:**

  - **Technique:** Engage in vigorous physical activity for a few minutes, like running in place or doing jumping jacks.

  - **How It Helps:** Intense exercise can help release built-up tension and trigger a rush of endorphins, improving your mood.

- **Paced Breathing:**

  - **Technique:** Practice slow, deep breathing by inhaling for a count of four, holding for four, and exhaling for four, then repeat.

  - **How It Helps:** Controlled breathing calms the nervous system and can help regulate your emotions during times of distress.

B. Self-Soothing Strategies: Creating a Safe Emotional Haven

Self-soothing strategies are techniques and practices that allow you to provide comfort and relief to yourself, much like a caring friend would do. These strategies are designed to create a safe emotional haven where you can find peace, regain your balance, and navigate through difficult emotions.

Here are some self-soothing techniques you can explore:

1. Positive Affirmations: Affirmations are positive statements that you repeat to yourself. They can counteract negative self-talk and help you build self-esteem. Here are 10 positive affirmations that you can use to boost your self-esteem and promote a positive mindset:

- I am capable of overcoming any challenges that come my way.

- I am resilient, and I bounce back from setbacks with strength.

- I believe in my abilities and trust myself to make the right decisions.

- I am deserving of love, respect, and happiness in my life.

- I am constantly growing and evolving into the best version of myself.

- I embrace change as an opportunity for growth and positive transformation.

- I am in control of my thoughts, and I choose to focus on positivity.

- I am surrounded by love and support from friends and family.

- I am grateful for each day and the opportunities it brings.

- I radiate confidence, and my self-worth is unshakable.

Feel free to choose the affirmations that resonate most with you and repeat them regularly to reinforce positive thinking and self-belief. Affirmations can be a powerful tool for building self-esteem and cultivating a positive outlook on life. Aim to repeat positive affirmations 10 times a day in front of the mirror.

2. Self-Care Rituals: Engaging in self-care activities can be incredibly soothing. Self-care is about prioritizing your well-being.

Here are ten examples of self-care rituals:

- Meditation and Mindfulness: Spend time meditating or practicing mindfulness to relax your mind and reduce stress.

- Warm Bath or Shower: Take a soothing bath or shower to unwind and refresh your body.

- Face Mask and Skincare: Pamper yourself with a facial mask and skincare routine to rejuvenate your skin.

- Reading: Escape into a good book or magazine to stimulate your imagination and relax your mind.

- Exercise: Engage in physical activity, whether it's yoga, jogging, or dancing, to boost your mood and energy levels.

- Journaling: Write down your thoughts, feelings, and goals to gain clarity and relieve emotional tension.

- Nature Walk or Hike: Connect with nature by going for a walk or hike in a park or natural setting.

- Listening to Music: Enjoy your favorite music or explore new tunes to lift your spirits.

- Aromatherapy: Use essential oils or scented candles to create a calming atmosphere at home.

- Artistic Expression: Engage in creative activities like painting, drawing, or crafting to express yourself and relax.

Remember that self-care is unique to each individual, so it's essential to find rituals that resonate with you and help you feel rejuvenated and balanced.

3. Use Your Senses: Your senses can be powerful tools for self-soothing. Consider activities like:

- Listening to Calming Music: Music has the power to evoke emotions and can be a source of comfort.

- Cuddling with a Soft Blanket or Stuffed Animal: The sensation of touch can be soothing and grounding.

- Savoring a Treat: Enjoying a small piece of chocolate or your favorite snack can provide a moment of pleasure.

4. Breathing Exercises: Deep, slow breathing techniques can calm your nervous system and reduce anxiety. Try inhaling deeply for a count of four, holding for four, and exhaling for four. Repeat this pattern.

5. Guided Imagery: Close your eyes and visualize a safe and serene place. This could be a peaceful beach, a cozy cabin in the woods, or any setting that makes you feel relaxed and secure.

6. Journaling: Writing down your thoughts and emotions can be a form of emotional release and self-reflection. It allows you to express yourself without judgment and gain insights into your feelings.

7. Mindfulness Meditation: Practicing mindfulness involves being fully present in the moment. It can help you observe your emotions without judgment and reduce their intensity.

C. Creating Your Safe Space

Consider creating a physical space in your home that promotes relaxation and self-soothing. This could be a cozy corner with soft cushions, soothing colors, and items that bring you comfort.

Remember, self-soothing is a skill that you can develop and customize to suit your unique needs. It's an act of self-compassion, allowing you to be kind and gentle with yourself during challenging times. Explore these strategies and discover what works best for you as you build your emotional resilience.

These Crisis Survival Skills, including the TIPP Skills and Self-Soothing Strategies, serve as your emergency toolkit for managing distressing moments. Remember, it's okay to reach out to trusted friends or adults for support when needed.

Skill Set 2: Pros and Cons of Distracting

Distracting is a common response when faced with intense emotions or distressing situations. Sometimes, it can be an effective way to temporarily shift your focus away from what's bothering you. However, not all forms of distraction are equally helpful, and it's essential to understand when this strategy can be beneficial and when it might not be the best choice.

The Pros of Distracting:

1. Immediate Relief: Distracting can offer immediate relief from emotional pain, giving you a breather from intense feelings.

2. Time for Calm: It allows you to create a buffer of time during which emotions might naturally subside or become more manageable.

3. Break from Overthinking: If you're stuck in a cycle of overthinking or negative self-talk, distraction can interrupt that pattern.

The Cons of Distracting:

1. Avoidance: Overusing distraction as a coping strategy can lead to avoidance of important emotions or issues, which can make them more challenging to address later.

2. Temporary Solution: It's a short-term solution and may not address the root causes of distress or provide long-lasting relief.

3. Possible Negative Outcomes: Depending on the distraction method chosen, it might lead to negative consequences, such as procrastination or neglecting responsibilities.

Finding Balance

The key to effective distraction is finding a balance. It's essential to recognize when distraction can be helpful in providing immediate relief, but also to be mindful of when it's masking deeper emotions or avoiding necessary problem-solving.

- *Scenario 1 (Helpful): You're feeling overwhelmed by a recent breakup, and your emotions are intense. You decide to watch a funny movie with friends to distract yourself from the pain and find some laughter.*

- *Scenario 2 (Not Helpful): You're facing a looming deadline for a school project, and the pressure is causing high levels of stress. Instead of working on the project, you repeatedly check your social media to escape the stress temporarily.*

- *Scenario 3 (Helpful): You've had a disagreement with a family member, and it has left you feeling upset. You decide to go for a long walk in the park to clear your mind and take a break from the tension at home.*

Scenario 4 (Not Helpful): You've been feeling overwhelmed by a series of challenging exams and academic pressures. Instead of studying or seeking help with your studies, you turn to video games to distract yourself. While playing games temporarily eases your stress, it doesn't address the underlying academic challenges you're facing. As a result, your academic performance continues to suffer, and the stress remains unresolved.

italicize and indent to match Scenario 1-3

Navigating Challenges Worksheet - Scenario Analysis

Consider each scenario and determine which techniques from Chapter 4 (Problem-Solving, Acceptance Strategies, or Distress Tolerance) could be applied to address the situation. Write down the techniques you think would be helpful for each scenario. Sample responses have been provided to help with the worksheet.

Scenario 1

You have a major school project due in a week, and you're feeling overwhelmed by the workload. You're not sure where to start, and you're anxious about the deadline.

Sample response

- **Problem-Solving:** *In this situation, I would apply problem-solving techniques from CBT. I can break down the project into smaller tasks, create a to-do list, and set specific deadlines for each task. This will help me organize my work and reduce the feeling of being overwhelmed. Additionally, I can seek help or guidance from a teacher or classmates if I have questions about the project.*

Scenario 2

You had a disagreement with a close friend, and it's been bothering you for days. You can't stop thinking about the argument and feel tense whenever you see your friend.

Sample Response

- ***Acceptance Strategies:*** *In this situation, I would apply acceptance strategies from ACT. Acceptance involves acknowledging that disagreements and conflicts are a normal part of relationships. I can practice being more accepting of the fact that conflicts happen, and it's okay. This can help me let go of the tension and negative thoughts associated with the argument. Additionally, I can use mindfulness techniques to stay present and reduce rumination about the disagreement.*

Scenario 3

You're facing a sudden and unexpected crisis in your life, and you're struggling to manage your emotions and thoughts.

Sample Response

- ***Distress Tolerance:*** *In this situation, I would apply distress tolerance techniques from DBT. When facing a crisis, it's important to have strategies to manage overwhelming emotions. I can use TIPP skills to quickly reduce emotional intensity. For example, I can try holding an ice cube in my hand or engaging in intense physical activity to help calm myself down. These techniques can provide immediate relief during a crisis.*

Scenario 4

You often find yourself ruminating on negative thoughts and self-criticism. It's challenging to break free from these patterns.

Sample Response

- **Acceptance Strategies:** *In this situation, I would continue to apply acceptance strategies ACT. Acceptance can also be helpful for self-criticism and negative thoughts. I can practice self-compassion and remind myself that everyone makes mistakes and has flaws. Additionally, I can use defusion techniques to distance myself from the negative thoughts and observe them without getting caught up in them.*

Scenario 5

You have a tendency to procrastinate when it comes to studying for exams, which increases your stress levels as deadlines approach.

Sample Response

- **Problem-Solving:** *In this situation, I would apply problem-solving techniques from CBT. To address procrastination, I can create a study schedule with specific study times and breaks. Setting goals and using time management strategies can help me stay on track. I can also use self-soothing strategies to manage any anxiety or stress related to studying.*

Scenario 6

You're experiencing a surge of intense anger after a disagreement with a family member. You need a way to calm down and regain control.

Sample Response

- ***Distress Tolerance:*** *In this situation, I would apply distress tolerance techniques from DBT When experiencing intense anger, it's important to find ways to calm down. I can use self-soothing strategies such as deep breathing or engaging in a calming activity like listening to music or going for a walk. These techniques can help me regain control of my emotions.*

Scenario 7

You're constantly worried about what others think of you, and this fear of judgment is affecting your self-esteem and social interactions.

Sample Response

- ***Acceptance Strategies:*** *In this situation, I would continue to apply acceptance strategies from ACT. Acceptance can help me let go of the need for constant approval from others. I can practice self-acceptance and remind myself that I am valuable regardless of others' opinions. Additionally, I can use mindfulness techniques to stay present in social interactions and reduce self-consciousness.*

Scenario 8

You have a busy schedule with multiple commitments, and it's challenging to balance everything without feeling stressed and overwhelmed.

Sample Response

- **Problem-Solving:** *In this situation, I would apply problem-solving techniques from CBT. To manage a busy schedule, I can create a prioritized to-do list and identify tasks that can be delegated or postponed. Setting clear goals and time management strategies can help me balance my commitments and reduce stress.*

Conclusion

In the journey of teenage life, challenges are as certain as the changing seasons. However, within the pages of this chapter, you've explored a treasure trove of skills and insights designed to help you navigate these challenges with resilience and wisdom. As we wrap up this chapter, let's reflect on the wealth of knowledge you've gained.

Problem-Solving (CBT) has empowered you to tackle obstacles head-on. You've learned to identify and define personal challenges, brainstorm creative solutions, evaluate options wisely, and craft practical action plans. The real-life scenarios and exercises have honed your problem-solving skills, making you a more effective and confident decision-maker.

Acceptance Strategies (ACT) have illuminated the path of embracing your emotions and experiences with grace. You've discovered the difference between acceptance and avoidance, delved into the concept of psychological flexibility, practiced defusion techniques, and learned the art of staying present. The practical exercises have equipped you to weave acceptance into your daily life, fostering resilience and emotional intelligence.

Distress Tolerance (DBT) has armed you with invaluable tools for managing overwhelming emotions and crisis situations. You've explored the TIPP skills, self-soothing strategies, and the balance between distraction's pros and cons. Additionally, you've begun assembling your personal Distress Tolerance Toolbox, ensuring that you're always prepared to face life's storms with courage.

As we conclude this chapter, remember that these skills are not merely theoretical knowledge but powerful tools you can apply in the real world. By combining problem-solving, acceptance, and distress tolerance skills, you'll become a master navigator of life's challenges. These skills empower you to thrive, not despite adversity but because of it.

So, dear teenager, as you turn the page, embrace the adventure that awaits. You're armed with the wisdom and skills needed to navigate challenges with resilience, compassion, and grace.

5

BUILDING STRONG CONNECTIONS

Introduction

Welcome to Chapter 5 of *Therapy Vibes*. This chapter is all about building awesome relationships, and we're diving deep into the world of making meaningful connections with others.

Have you ever wondered how to communicate better with your friends, family, or even new people you meet? Well, you're in the right place! In this chapter, we're going to learn cool tricks and techniques to help you build and maintain healthy and fulfilling relationships.

We're mixing up a special recipe for this chapter. We've got three familiar ingredients: Interpersonal Effectiveness from Dialectical Behavior Therapy (DBT), Assertiveness Training from Cognitive Behavioral Therapy (CBT), and Creating a Support System from Acceptance and Commitment Therapy (ACT). These three ingredients together will give you a superpower – the ability to create amazing connections with people.

Let's get started by understanding the first ingredient: *Interpersonal Effectiveness.* Think of it as your map for navigating social situations. We'll show you how to set goals for your interactions, improve the quality of your relationships, and make sure you always respect yourself, no matter what.

Next up, we're going to talk about *Assertiveness Training*, which is like your secret communication weapon. Being assertive doesn't mean being pushy or too quiet – it's all about expressing your thoughts, feelings, and needs in a way that's clear and respectful. You'll learn how to communicate like a pro, set boundaries, and stand up for yourself.

Lastly, we'll explore the art of *Creating a Support System*. Your support network is like your superhero team. We'll help you find the right people or groups who share your values and can support you on your journey. You'll also discover how to talk to them about what you need and want from these relationships.

Throughout this chapter, you'll have chances to practice these skills in real-life scenarios, so you'll be ready to use them in your everyday life. Remember, building strong connections is like building a house – it takes time and effort, but it's totally worth it!

So, get ready to learn some fantastic relationship-building skills that will help you connect with others in a way that feels true to you. Let's jump in and explore the world of building strong and meaningful connections!

Section 1: Interpersonal Effectiveness (DBT)

Unlocking the Power of Interpersonal Effectiveness

Welcome to Section 1, where we'll dive into the world of *Interpersonal Effectiveness*. But wait, you might be wondering, what's DBT, and why is it a big deal when it comes to building stronger and healthier relationships? Well, let's unravel the mystery!

Dialectical Behavior Therapy (DBT) is like your personal guide to mastering the art of interpersonal effectiveness. It's not just a bunch of fancy therapy techniques; it's a practical approach to building healthier, happier relationships.

Think of it this way: Without these interpersonal skills, your interactions with others might look very different. Let's explore some sample scenarios to see what could happen without these skills:

- **Communicate Clearly:** Imagine you have a great idea for a group project at school, but you struggle to explain it clearly to your classmates. Without the skill of clear communication, your idea might get lost in translation, and your project could suffer from confusion and misunderstandings.

- **Understand Others:** Picture this: A friend seems upset, but you can't quite figure out why. Without the ability to understand others' emotions, you might miss important signals and not offer the support your friend needs, causing frustration and distance in the friendship.

- **Resolve Conflicts:** Suppose you and a family member have a disagreement about something important. Without conflict resolution skills, your arguments might escalate, and you could both end up feeling hurt and misunderstood instead of finding a constructive solution.

- **Set Boundaries:** Let's say someone keeps borrowing your things without asking, and it's starting to bother you. Without the skill of setting boundaries, you might feel uncomfortable but not know how to express your feelings. This could lead to ongoing frustration and resentment in your relationship.

- **Make Values-Based Choices:** Imagine you're invited to a party, but you have an important study session planned. Without the ability to make values-based choices, you might feel torn and unsure about what to do. You might end up making a decision that doesn't align with your long-term goals and values.

In short, without these interpersonal skills, your interactions could be marked by miscommunication, misunderstandings, unresolved conflicts, discomfort, and choices that don't align with your values. Your relationships may suffer, leading to frustration, stress, and a sense of disconnection.

DBT is here to change that by providing you with the tools you need to handle these situations more effectively, ensuring your relationships are marked by clarity, empathy, resolution, respect, and alignment with your values. Throughout this section, we'll delve deeper into these skills, helping you unlock your social superpowers and take your relationships to the next level. Get ready to embark on this exciting journey!

Objective Effectiveness: Achieving Your Interpersonal Goals

Objective Effectiveness is all about setting clear goals for your interactions and using practical strategies to achieve them. Imagine you're playing a game. To win, you need to know the rules and the goal. The same goes for your interactions with people – having clear objectives is like knowing your game plan.

- **Sample Scenario 1**

  - **Asking for Help with Homework:** Let's say you're struggling with a school assignment. Your objective might be to ask a classmate for help, ensuring that you clearly understand the concept you're studying.

- **Sample Scenario 2**

  - **Resolving a Misunderstanding:** If you've had a disagreement with a friend, your goal could be to clarify the misunderstanding and restore your friendship to its usual harmony.

- **Sample Scenario 3**

  - **Family Decision-Making:** In a family discussion about where to go on vacation, your objective might be to advocate for a destination you've always wanted to visit while ensuring that everyone's preferences are considered.

- **Sample Scenario 4**

  - **Job Interview:** When you're in a job interview, your goal could be to impress the interviewer by highlighting your qualifications and demonstrating why you're the best fit for the position.

- **Sample Scenario 5**

  - **Team Project:** Working on a group project, your objective might be to lead the team effectively by setting clear roles and expectations, ensuring that the project is completed successfully and on time.

Once you have your objectives in place, it's time to put your strategies into action.

Mastering Interpersonal Interaction

In this section, we'll explore practical strategies for achieving your objectives during various interpersonal interactions. These strategies are essential for effective communication, building rapport, and resolving conflicts. Let's dive deep into each one:

Effective Communication

Effective communication is the foundation of successful interactions. It involves not only expressing yourself clearly but also actively listening to others. Here's a step-by-step breakdown of effective communication:

1. Active Listening

- When actively listening, focus your attention on the speaker.

- Avoid interrupting and let the person finish speaking.

- Use non-verbal cues like nodding to show you're engaged.

- After they've finished, summarize what they've said to ensure you understood correctly.

Sample Scenario: You're in a group project meeting, and your classmate is sharing their ideas. You practice active listening by maintaining eye contact, not interrupting, and summarizing their key points.

2. Clear Expression

- Express your thoughts, feelings, and intentions clearly and assertively.

- Use "I" statements to express your feelings and thoughts without accusing or blaming others.

- Avoid aggressive or passive communication styles.

Sample Scenario: During a discussion about project roles, you say, "I believe I can contribute most effectively by handling the research aspect of the project," clearly expressing your intention.

Building Rapport

Building rapport is about creating a positive and comfortable atmosphere in your interactions. It helps establish connections and open lines of communication. Here's how to do it:

1. Friendly and Approachable Demeanor

- Be warm and welcoming when you meet someone.

- Smile and use open body language to convey friendliness.

- Show interest in their well-being and experiences.

Sample Scenario: You meet a new student at school. You smile, introduce yourself, and ask about their interests, making them feel welcome.

2. Empathy:

- Put yourself in the other person's shoes to understand their feelings and perspective.

- Acknowledge their emotions, even if you don't agree with them.

- Show empathy by saying, "I understand how you might feel that way."

Sample Scenario: Your friend is upset about a recent test score. Instead of dismissing their feelings, you say, "I understand how you might be disappointed, but we can work on improving together."

Conflict Resolution Techniques

Conflict is a natural part of relationships, but how you handle it can make all the difference. These techniques can help you resolve conflicts peacefully and maintain positive relationships:

1. Staying Calm

- Keep your emotions in check during disagreements.

- Take deep breaths and count to ten if necessary to avoid reacting impulsively.

- Stay focused on the issue at hand, not on personal attacks.

Sample Scenario: You and your sibling are arguing over who gets to use the computer. Instead of yelling, you take a deep breath and calmly state your reasons.

2. Using "I" Statements

- Express your feelings and thoughts using "I" statements to avoid blaming and defensiveness.

- Formulate your statement as "I feel [emotion] when [specific situation] because [reason]."

Sample Scenario: When resolving a disagreement with a friend about weekend plans, you say, "I feel disappointed when our plans change last minute because I was looking forward to spending time with you."

3. Seeking Common Ground

- Identify areas of agreement and shared interests.

- Collaborate to find mutually beneficial solutions.

- Focus on what you both want to achieve rather than what you disagree on.

Sample Scenario: You and your friend have different opinions on a school project. By seeking common ground, you find aspects of the project that you both value and can work together on.

Mastering these strategies will empower you to excel in various interpersonal interactions, whether in personal relationships, academic settings, or the workplace. Practice these skills regularly, and they will become valuable tools in your toolkit for building harmonious connections and resolving conflicts effectively.

Relationship Effectiveness: Nurturing Meaningful Connections

Welcome to the section on Relationship Effectiveness, where you'll explore the art of nurturing meaningful connections with others. While some skills may overlap with Objective Effectiveness, this section delves deeper into the broader aspects of relationships and how to make them more fulfilling and healthy.

Understanding the Importance of Relationship Effectiveness

Let's talk about why having cool, healthy relationships is such a big deal for teens like you. It's not just about having friends or getting along with family; it's about how these connections make your life better.

Different Types of Relationships: Your Social Mix

Think about all the people in your life - your family, friends, and maybe even someone special. These are the folks who make up your social mix, and they come in different flavors:

- **Family Relationships:** These are the folks you share a home with. It's your parents, siblings, and maybe even your extended family. They're like your lifelong buddies, even if you have moments of sibling rivalry!

- **Friendships:** Friends are your chosen crew. They're the people you hang out with, laugh with, and rely on. Friends are like the family you get to pick!

- **Romantic Relationships:** If you've got a crush or someone you're dating, that's your romantic relationship. It's the stuff of movies, butterflies, and heart emojis.

The Good Vibes of Healthy Relationships: Why It Matters

Now, let's get to the juicy part - why having healthier relationships is awesome for you:

- **More Happiness:** When you have good people around, you're likely to feel happier. They're there for fun times, inside jokes, and creating happy memories together.

- **Less Stress:** Stress can be a real downer, but healthy relationships act like a stress-busting superhero. When things get tough, you've got someone to lean on, making problems feel smaller.

- **Better Mental Health:** Healthy relationships can boost your mental well-being. Having friends who care about you and listen can make you feel less alone and more understood.

- **Physical Perks:** Believe it or not, healthy relationships can even have physical perks. Lower stress levels can help your immune system stay strong, so you stay healthier.

- **Personal Growth:** Good relationships push you to grow and become a better you. They make you think, feel, and learn new things about yourself and others.

Remember, these relationships aren't just about having fun - they're a big part of what makes you, well, you! So, as you explore the world of relationships, keep in mind how they can make your teen life richer and more exciting.

Building Trust and Connection: Strengthening the Relationship Foundation

Alright, let's dive into the heart of this section - building trust and connection in your relationships. Whether it's with family, friends, or someone special, trust is like the secret ingredient that makes relationships solid. We're going to explore some awesome strategies to make this happen:

1. Transparency and Honesty: Keeping It Real

The Power of Honesty

Honesty is like the secret sauce that adds flavor to your relationships. It's all about being real and truthful in your interactions. When you're honest, you're like a reliable guide in the relationship journey, and here's why it's so powerful:

Why Honesty Matters

Being honest is like opening the door to trust and understanding in your relationships. When you're truthful, you show that you respect others enough to share your real thoughts and feelings. It's a way of saying, "I trust you enough to be myself around you."

The Magic of Gentle Honesty

Honesty doesn't mean being brutally blunt or hurtful. It's about sharing your thoughts and feelings in a way that's kind and considerate. Think of it as a friendly guide helping you navigate tricky conversations.

Now, let's dive into an example to see how the power of honesty works in a real-life situation:

Positive Example - The Power of Honesty

Imagine your friend asks if you like their new haircut. You take a moment to consider your response because you want to be both honest and caring. So, you say, "I appreciate your new style, and it's great to see you trying something different." In this case, your honesty is gentle and respectful of their feelings.

Counterexample - When Honesty Falls Short

On the flip side, let's say you responded with a dishonest compliment like, "It's amazing!" when you actually dislike the haircut. Your friend later discovers your true opinion and feels hurt because they thought you were being truthful.

---

2. Being Open: Sharing Your Real Self

Being open is like unlocking the treasure chest of your thoughts and feelings, allowing others to get to know the real you. It's all about freely expressing yourself and being willing to let people in on what's going on inside your head and heart. So, why is being open such a big deal in relationships? Let's explore:

Why Being Open Matters

When you're open, you create a bridge of connection between you and others. It's like saying, "I trust you enough to share my thoughts and feelings." Being open helps people understand you better and allows them to connect with the real you.

The Art of Expressing Yourself

Being open doesn't mean sharing everything all at once or oversharing. It's about finding the right balance between what you keep to yourself and what you're comfortable sharing. Think of it as a way to paint a clearer picture of who you are.

Now, let's dive into an example to see how being open plays out in real life:

Positive Example - Being Open:

Your sibling asks how your day went, and you decide to be open about it. You share both the exciting and challenging parts of your day. You express your feelings openly, saying, "I had a great time hanging out with friends after school, but I also struggled with a math quiz." By being open, you make it easier for your sibling to connect with you on a deeper level.

Counterexample - When Closed Off:

On the flip side, let's say you respond with a vague, "It was fine," without sharing any details. Your sibling feels like you're closed off and not interested in sharing with them. This can make it challenging to connect because they don't know what's going on in your life.

3. Building Trustworthiness: The Foundation of Trust

Trustworthiness is like the rock-solid foundation upon which you build your relationships. It's all about being someone others can rely on, count on, and trust. So, what's the big deal about trustworthiness, and why does it matter in your relationships? Let's dive in:

Why Trustworthiness Matters

When you're trustworthy, you become a dependable and consistent presence in others' lives. It's like saying, "You can count on me." Trustworthiness fosters feelings of security and reliability, making people feel safe in your company.

The Building Blocks of Trustworthiness

Trustworthiness isn't something you're born with; it's something you develop through your actions and behaviors. It includes qualities like honesty, reliability, and keeping your word.

Now, let's explore an example to see how trustworthiness can make a difference in real-life situations:

Positive Example - Building Trustworthiness:
Imagine you promise your friend that you'll help them with a school project. You make a commitment and set aside dedicated time to work on the project together. By keeping your promise and following through, you demonstrate your integrity and reliability. Your friend knows they can trust your word in the future.

Counterexample - When Trustworthiness Falters:
On the flip side, let's say you promise to help your friend with the project but then bail out at the last minute without a valid reason. Your friend feels let down and questions whether they can trust your word in the future. This can strain the relationship because trustworthiness wasn't upheld.

Reliability and Consistency: Building Trust Through Dependability

In this section, we're going to explore the super important qualities of reliability and consistency. Think of them as the building blocks of trust in your relationships. They're like the secret sauce that makes your connections stronger and more dependable. Let's dive in:

1. What Reliability Means: Being the Go-To Person

- **Positive Example - What Reliability Means**

  - Imagine your friend knows that when they need someone to talk to, you're always there to listen and offer support, no matter the time or situation. Whether it's a late-night chat or a crisis, they can rely on you to be present and supportive.

- **Counterexample - When Reliability Falters**

  - Now, picture a scenario where your friend reaches out during a tough time, but you're consistently unavailable or dismissive. They feel like you're not reliable when they need you most, and it strains the trust in your relationship.

2. Being There When It Counts: Consistent Support Matters

- **Positive Example - Being There When It Counts**

  - Your sibling is going through a difficult breakup, and you offer your support by being present. You provide a shoulder to cry on, lend a listening ear, and offer comforting words. Your consistent support helps your sibling feel cared for during their challenging time.

- **Counterexample - Missing in Action**

  - In a different scenario, your sibling confides in you about their breakup, but you brush off their feelings and change the subject, leaving them feeling unsupported. Your inconsistency in being there for them when they needed you can create a gap in your relationship.

3. Consistency Is Key: Building Trust Through Predictability

- **Positive Example - Consistency Is Key**

  - In your friendships, you always keep your promises and maintain a consistent level of support and care. Your friends know they can rely on you to be the same trustworthy person every day. This consistency helps strengthen your bonds.

- **Counterexample - The Unpredictable Friend**

  - On the flip side, imagine your behavior varies greatly from day to day. Your friends struggle to predict how you'll react or if you'll follow through with your commitments. This unpredictability can lead to uncertainty and strained friendships.

Respect for Boundaries: Navigating Personal Space

Boundaries are like the invisible lines that define your personal space and comfort zones in relationships. In this section, we'll explore the art of respecting boundaries—both yours and others'. It's all about creating a safe and respectful environment where everyone feels comfortable and valued. Let's dig in:

1. What Are Boundaries? Defining Personal Space

- **Positive Example - What Are Boundaries?**

  - Imagine your friend tells you they need some alone time to recharge after a hectic week. You respect their boundary and don't pressure them to hang out. In the positive example, you understand and honor your friend's need for alone time. By respecting their boundary, you show that you value their feelings and autonomy.

- **Counterexample - Crossing Boundaries**

  - On the flip side, let's say you ignore your friend's request for alone time and keep insisting they join in on group activities. Your friend feels overwhelmed and disregarded. In the counterexample, you disregard your friend's boundary, making them feel like their needs are not important. This can lead to discomfort and strain in the relationship because boundaries are not being respected.

2. Respecting Others' Boundaries: Building Trust Through Respect

- **Positive Example - Respecting Others' Boundaries**

  - Your sibling asks you not to touch their belongings without permission. You honor their request and ask before borrowing anything, showing respect for their personal space. In the positive example, you demonstrate respect for your sibling's belongings by asking for permission before borrowing. This builds trust and shows consideration for their feelings.

- **Counterexample - Disregarding Boundaries**

  - On the other hand, let's say you frequently borrow your sibling's things without asking, assuming it's okay. Your sibling feels frustrated and like their boundaries are being violated. The counterexample illustrates a lack of respect for your sibling's boundaries. Ignoring their requests can lead to frustration and erode trust in the relationship because their personal space and possessions are not being respected.

3. Setting Your Own Boundaries: Building Healthy Relationship

- **Positive Example - Setting Your Own Boundaries**

  - You let your friends know that you need some downtime on weekends to focus on self-care and personal interests. They respect your boundary and plan activities accordingly. In the positive example, you communicate your needs to your friends, and they respect your request for downtime. This leads to stronger connections because your friends understand and support your well-being.

- **Counterexample - Neglecting Your Boundaries**

  - On the contrary, let's say you neglect to communicate your need for downtime, leaving your friends to make plans for every weekend. You feel overwhelmed and unable to take care of your well-being. In this counterexample, the absence of clear boundaries can strain your mental and emotional health.

Managing Conflict and Resolving Differences: Navigating Relationship Bumps

Conflict is like the bump in the road of relationships. It's bound to happen, but how you handle it can make all the difference. In this section, we're diving into the world of effective conflict resolution. It's all about turning conflicts into opportunities for growth and stronger connections. Let's dive in:

Active Problem-Solving: Finding Solutions Together

- **Positive Example - Active Problem-Solving**

  - Imagine you and your friend have a disagreement about where to go for a group outing. Instead of arguing, you sit down, discuss options, and find a solution that everyone agrees on. In this positive example, you and your friend put your heads together to resolve the conflict constructively. This approach strengthens your connection because you're collaborating rather than arguing.

- **Counterexample - Unproductive Arguments**

  - On the flip side, let's say you and your friend engage in a heated argument, each insisting on your own choice for the outing. The disagreement escalates, and no solution is reached. In this counterexample, the conflict escalates because active problem-solving is absent, resulting in frustration and tension between you and your friend.

De-escalation Techniques: Maintaining Constructive Conversations

- **Positive Example - De-escalation Techniques**

  - Picture a scenario where tensions rise during a conversation with your sibling. Instead of reacting with anger, you take a deep breath, use calming language, and listen actively to understand their perspective. In this positive example, you manage to calm the situation by using de-escalation strategies. This helps prevent conflicts from spiraling out of control.

- **Counterexample - Escalation and Hostility**

  - Now, consider a situation where you react to your sibling's comment with anger, raising your voice and responding with hostility. The conversation becomes more heated, and understanding is lost. In this counterexample, the conflict intensifies due to a lack of de-escalation techniques, leading to strained relations with your sibling.

Forgiveness and Repair: Healing After Conflict

- **Positive Example - Forgiveness and Repair**

  - Think of a time when a friend unintentionally hurt your feelings. After discussing the issue openly, your friend sincerely apologizes, and you choose to forgive them. Your friendship grows stronger as a result. In this positive example, you and your friend engage in this process, leading to stronger trust and a deeper connection.

- **Counterexample - Lingering Resentment**

  - In contrast, imagine your friend hurts your feelings, but neither of you addresses the issue. Resentment builds, and the friendship becomes strained. In this counterexample, the conflict remains unresolved, negatively impacting your friendship.

Recognizing Toxic Relationships: Setting Healthy Boundaries

- **Positive Example - Recognizing Toxic Relationships**

  - Picture a situation where you notice signs of an unhealthy friendship characterized by constant criticism and manipulation. You decide to set boundaries and limit your interactions with this friend. In this positive example, you prioritize your well-being by setting boundaries with a toxic friend, demonstrating self-care and self-respect.

- **Counterexample - Ignoring Red Flags**

  - On the other hand, consider a scenario where you disregard warning signs of a toxic relationship and continue to engage with a friend who consistently disrespects your boundaries. The negativity takes a toll on your emotional health. In this counterexample, neglecting to set boundaries in a toxic friendship can lead to emotional distress and strain.

Top 10 Signs of a Toxic Relationship

1. *Constant Criticism*: Your partner constantly criticizes your appearance, intelligence, or choices, saying things like, "You're so stupid; you can't do anything right."

2. *Control and Possessiveness:* They monitor your phone and social media, demanding to know your whereabouts, or saying, "You can't hang out with them; I don't trust them."

3. *Jealousy and Insecurity:* They become excessively jealous when you spend time with other people, asking, "Why were you talking to them? Are you attracted to them?"

4. *Manipulation:* They guilt-trip you into doing things you don't want to do, saying, "If you loved me, you'd do this for me."

5. *Isolation:* They discourage you from seeing your friends or family, saying, "You don't need them; you have me."

6. *Lack of Respect for Boundaries*: They invade your privacy by going through your personal belongings or showing up unannounced despite your objections.

7. *Verbal or Physical Abuse:* They scream at you, call you names, or physically harm you, leaving you frightened and hurt.

8. *Constant Negativity:* Every interaction with them is filled with criticism and negativity, leaving you emotionally drained, and they often say, "You're never good enough."

9. *Dependency:* They rely on you for emotional support, financial stability, or even basic daily tasks, making you feel overwhelmed and trapped.

10. *Lack of Accountability:* They blame you or others for their mistakes, refusing to take responsibility, and saying, "It's your fault; you made me do this."

Recognizing these signs and taking action to set healthy boundaries is crucial for maintaining your emotional and mental well-being in any relationship.

Nurturing Positive Connections: Building and Sustaining Fulfilling Relationships

- **Positive Example - Nurturing Positive Connections:**

Think of a time when you actively worked on building a positive connection with a new friend. You invested time in getting to know them, shared experiences, and maintained open communication, resulting in a rewarding friendship. In this positive example, you put in the effort to foster a new friendship, leading to a fulfilling and enriching connection.

- **Counterexample - Neglecting Relationship Building:**

In contrast, imagine a scenario where you neglected to invest time and effort in maintaining connections with your existing friends. Over time, the relationships became distant and unfulfilling. In this counterexample, the lack of effort in maintaining friendships resulted in distant and unfulfilling relationships.

Nurturing Self-Respect in Relationships

In the world of building solid connections with others, there's a super important thing many peeps forget about, and that's self-respect. It ain't just about how others treat you; it's about how you treat yourself and make sure your needs, boundaries, and vibes are all good. In this section, we're gonna break down why self-respect is such a big deal in relationships and give you some rad tools and tips to keep it going strong.

Understanding Self-Respect's Role: The Backbone of Awesome Relationships

Before we jump into the nitty-gritty stuff, you gotta get why self-respect is like the backbone of having awesome relationships and feeling good about yourself. If you wanna build killer connections with others, you've gotta start by building up your own self-respect.

- **Building Healthy Connections:** Think of self-respect as the solid foundation of a skyscraper. Without it, your relationships might crumble. When you respect yourself, you set the standard for how others should treat you. It's like telling the world, "I deserve to be treated with kindness and consideration." When you have self-respect, you naturally attract people who value and respect you too. It's like building a squad of awesome peeps who lift you up.

- **Staying True to You:** Self-respect is like your inner compass. It helps you stay true to yourself and your values, even when you're in a relationship. You won't compromise your beliefs or change who you are just to fit in or make someone else happy. You stay authentically you, and that's pretty darn cool.

- **Less Drama, More Peace:** When you've got self-respect, you're less likely to get caught up in drama or toxic relationships. You know your worth, and you won't settle for less. It's like having a forcefield that keeps negativity at bay, and that means more peace and positivity in your life.

- **Boosting Confidence:** Having self-respect gives your confidence a major boost. You walk taller, talk confidently, and hold your head high. This not only makes you more attractive to others but also helps you achieve your goals and dreams.

- **Overall Well-Being:** It's not just about relationships; self-respect impacts your whole vibe. When you respect yourself, you make choices that support your well-being. You're more likely to prioritize self-care, set and achieve goals, and lead a fulfilling life.

So, in a nutshell, self-respect is like the secret sauce for building healthy, happy relationships and living your best life. It's all about setting the stage for respect, authenticity, and positivity in every aspect of your world.

Setting and Communicating Boundaries Like a Pro

Alright, so picture this: Setting boundaries is like creating your personal space bubble. It's all about letting peeps know what's cool with you and what's not, and guess what? It's totally cool to have boundaries. In this section, we're gonna help you become a boundary-setting ninja, and we're doing it in a way that's all about keeping the good vibes rollin' in your relationships.

Assertive Boundary Establishment: Keeping Your Respect Game Strong

Now, when it comes to setting boundaries, you gotta do it with confidence. It's like telling the world, "Hey, this is me, and here's what's important to me." But doing it without feeling all awkward can be a bit tricky, right? No worries, we've got your back. Here's how to do it:

- **Know What You're About:** First things first, you gotta know what's important to you. What are your values? What makes you feel comfortable or uncomfortable in different situations? Understanding your own wants and needs is key.

- **Speak Up, Don't Bottle Up:** Setting boundaries is all about communication. When something doesn't sit right with you, don't keep it locked up inside. Let the other person know in a chill and respectful way. It's not about being bossy; it's about expressing yourself.

- **Use "I" Statements:** This is a neat trick. Instead of saying, "You make me feel..." or "You should do this," use "I" statements like, "I feel uncomfortable when..." or "I need..." It's a non-confrontational way to express your boundaries without making the other person defensive.

- **Stick to Your Guns:** Once you've set a boundary, stick to it. Don't let anyone push you around or make you feel bad for having your limits. Remember, your boundaries are there to protect your well-being.

Example Time

Imagine you've got a friend who always borrows your stuff without asking, and it's starting to bug you. Here's how you can set a boundary:

- **Not-So-Great Way:** "You always take my things without permission, and it's annoying. Stop doing that!"

- **Better Way with "I" Statement:** "Hey, I've noticed that sometimes my things are borrowed without asking, and it makes me feel uncomfortable. Can we chat about this and figure out a way to make sure we're cool with sharing stuff?"

See the difference? Using an "I" statement keeps things chill and respectful while expressing your boundary.

Setting boundaries is all about making your relationships healthier and more respectful. It's like drawing a line in the sand and saying, "This is me, and I'm keeping it real."

Balancing Self-Respect and Compassion: Finding Your Groove

Now, let's talk about finding that sweet spot between showing respect to yourself and spreading some good ol' compassion to others. It's like dancing to your own beat while keeping the harmony in your relationships.

Self-Compassion in Interactions: Be Your Own Bestie

Ever heard of self-compassion? It's basically being your own bestie. You know how you're kind and understanding to your friends when they mess up? Well, it's time to treat yourself the same way. Here's the deal:

- **Be Kind to You:** Self-compassion is about cutting yourself some slack. When you make a mistake or face a tough situation, instead of being hard on yourself, treat yourself with kindness. It's like giving yourself a warm hug and saying, "It's gonna be okay."

- **Accept Imperfections:** We're all human, and we all goof up sometimes. Embrace your imperfections and know that they don't define you. It's all part of the awesome journey called life.

- **Boosting Self-Esteem:** When you practice self-compassion, your self-esteem gets a major boost. You feel more confident and ready to take on any challenge. Plus, it's easier to spread positivity to others when you're feeling good about yourself.

Navigating Conflict with Grace: Keeping the Good Vibes Alive

Alright, let's get real—conflicts happen. But guess what? You can handle them like a pro without losing your self-respect. It's all about keeping those good vibes alive:

- **Stay Cool, Calm, and Collected:** When a conflict pops up, the key is to stay chill. Keep your emotions in check, take deep breaths, and remember that shouting and drama won't solve anything.

- **Active Listening:** Instead of going on the offense, practice active listening. Hear out the other person's side, and they're more likely to do the same for you. It's like creating a bridge of understanding.

- **Seek Common Ground:** Find common ground or compromise to resolve the issue. It's not about winning or losing; it's about finding a solution that works for both sides.

Example Time

Imagine you and your bestie had a falling out because of a misunderstanding. Here's how you can balance self-respect and compassion:

- **Not-So-Great Way:** "You messed up big time, and I don't want to talk to you ever again!"

- **Better Way with Self-Compassion:** "Hey, I know we had a rough patch, and I felt hurt by what happened. But I also understand that we all make mistakes. Let's chat and figure this out together."

See how you can address the conflict while being compassionate and respectful?

Balancing self-respect and compassion is like finding the perfect harmony in a song. It makes your relationships more epic and keeps you feeling good about yourself.

Interpersonal Effectiveness Worksheet: Building Stronger Relationships

In this worksheet, we're diving into some awesome exercises to help you boost your interpersonal skills and create healthier, more fulfilling relationships. Let's get started!

Exercise 1: Self-Reflection on Interpersonal Skills

Take a moment to reflect on your own interpersonal skills and how they impact your relationships. Be honest with yourself, and remember, we're all a work in progress. Use the space below to jot down your thoughts:

1. How would you describe your current interpersonal skills? (e.g., communication, active listening, conflict resolution)

Sample Response: *I think I'm pretty good at listening to my friends, but I sometimes struggle with expressing my own thoughts and feelings clearly.*

2. Can you think of a recent situation where your interpersonal skills played a role in the outcome? Describe what happened and how your skills influenced it.

Sample Response: *Last week, I had an argument with my sibling. I got really defensive and didn't listen to their side of the story, which made things worse.*

3. What do you think are your strengths when it comes to building relationships with others?

Sample Response: *I'm a good listener, and I'm usually there for my friends when they need me.*

4. What areas do you feel you need to improve in when it comes to interpersonal skills?

Sample Response: *I need to work on expressing myself more clearly and not getting defensive during conflicts.*

Exercise 2: Setting Boundaries Like a Pro

Setting boundaries is key to maintaining self-respect and healthy relationships. Let's practice setting and communicating boundaries with confidence. Fill in the blanks:

1. A boundary I want to set for myself is:

Sample Response: *A boundary I want to set for myself is not lending out my belongings without asking first.*

2. Why is this boundary important to me? How does it protect my self-respect and well-being?

Sample Response: *This boundary is important because it helps me feel respected and ensures my things are treated with care. It protects my self-respect by letting others know what's okay and what's not.*

3. How can I assertively communicate this boundary to others without feeling awkward?

Sample Response: *I can say something like, "Hey, I've noticed that sometimes my things are borrowed without asking, and it makes me feel uncomfortable. Can we chat about this and figure out a way to make sure we're cool with sharing stuff?"*

Exercise 3: Conflict Resolution Practice

Conflict happens, but handling it with grace and respect can strengthen your relationships. Imagine you had a conflict with a friend. Use this space to plan out how you'd resolve it while preserving your self-respect:

1. Describe the conflict and why it's bothering you.

Sample Response: *My friend and I argued about who should do the project presentation. It's bothering me because we both want to do well, but we can't agree on who should present.*

2. How can you stay calm and collected during the conversation?

Sample Response: *I can take deep breaths and remind myself that it's okay to have different opinions.*

3. Use "I" statements to express your feelings and needs.

Sample Response: *"I feel like we both have valuable ideas for the presentation, and I want us to find a way to work together that feels fair to both of us."*

4. How can you seek common ground or compromise to resolve the conflict?

Sample Response: *We can discuss our ideas and see if there's a way to incorporate both of our strengths into the presentation. Maybe we can alternate speaking during the presentation.*

Remember, these exercises are all about growth and improvement. Keep practicing, and you'll become a pro at boosting your interpersonal effectiveness and building stronger relationships.

Section 2: Assertiveness Training (CBT): Building Confidence in Communication

Unlocking the Power of Assertiveness with CBT

In this section, we're diving deep into assertiveness training, and guess what? It's the perfect companion for Cognitive Behavioral Therapy (CBT). Let's explore how these two concepts work together to supercharge your communication skills and boost your confidence.

The Connection Between Assertiveness and CBT

Assertiveness is like a bridge between your thoughts and behaviors, and it plays a crucial role in CBT. Here's how assertiveness puts CBT concepts into action:

1. **Changing Negative Thoughts:** Assertiveness helps you express your thoughts and needs more clearly, which can prevent misunderstandings and conflicts that often arise from miscommunication.

2. **Behavioral Activation:** Being assertive means you actively participate in your interactions, which aligns with the behavioral activation principles of CBT.

3. **Replacing Negative Behaviors:** Assertiveness replaces passive or aggressive communication styles with a balanced and respectful approach, aligning with CBT's goal of behavior modification.

By mastering assertiveness you're actively incorporating CBT principles into your interpersonal interactions, leading to more positive and effective communication.

Let's explore some of the superpowers that come with assertiveness:

- **Healthier Relationships:** When you communicate assertively, you build trust and respect with others. It's like a recipe for creating stronger connections.

- **Confidence Boost:** Assertiveness helps you feel more confident and in control of your interactions. You'll rock that "I've got this" vibe.

- **Conflict Resolution Pro:** Assertive folks are like the superheroes of conflict resolution. You can tackle issues head-on without creating more drama.

- **Self-Respect:** Assertiveness is all about standing up for yourself in a respectful way. It's like wearing a cape of self-respect.

Assertiveness Skills: The Art of Speaking Your Truth

Now, it's time to learn the nitty-gritty of assertiveness. These skills are like your trusty sidekicks in the world of communication:

Expressing Thoughts: The Art of Clear and Confident Communication

Before we dive into the steps of expressing your thoughts assertively, let's talk about why it's so important. Imagine a world where everyone understands each other clearly and confidently expresses their ideas. That world would be filled with effective communication, fewer misunderstandings, and stronger connections.

Expressing your thoughts is like being a language superhero—it allows you to share your ideas, contribute to discussions, and ensure your voice is heard. It's about communicating with confidence and making sure your valuable input isn't lost in the crowd.

Now, let's break down the steps to help you master the art of expressing your thoughts clearly and confidently.

Step 1: Clarity is Key

- Before speaking up, take a moment to organize your thoughts about your message and how you want to express it clearly.

Step 2: Use "I" Statements *(This step has come up several times already, but it's genuinely important)*

- Instead of making general statements, use "I" statements to express your thoughts, ensuring your message is about your perspective and feelings.

Step 3: Active Listening

- After sharing your thoughts, actively listen to the responses and questions from others, showing that you value their input.

Sample Scenarios

1. Classroom Contribution

- Step 1: Before speaking up, take a moment to organize your thoughts about your project idea and how it could benefit the group.

- Step 2: Instead of blurting out your idea, say, "I have an idea for our science project that I think could make it even better."

- Step 3: After sharing your idea, actively listen to your classmates' responses and questions, showing that you value their input.

2. Group Decision-Making

- Step 1: Take a moment to think about where you'd like to go and why it's your preference.

- Step 2: Instead of saying, "Let's go to the movies," say, "I'd really like to go to the movies because I love watching films on the big screen."

- Step 3: After sharing your preference, actively listen to your friends' opinions and consider their input in the decision.

3. Family Discussion

- Step 1: Reflect on the destination you'd like to propose and why it would be a great choice.

- Step 2: Instead of saying, "We should go to the beach," say, "I think going to the beach would be fantastic because we can relax and have fun by the ocean."

- Step 3: After sharing your suggestion, actively listen to your family members' thoughts and preferences to facilitate a constructive discussion.

Sharing Feelings: The Art of Emotional Expression

Sharing your feelings is like opening a window to your heart. It's a powerful way to connect with others on a deeper level and let them see the real you. In this section, we're going to explore the art of emotional expression and why it's a game-changer in your relationships.

Imagine a world where everyone feels safe to express their emotions, where understanding and empathy flow freely. It's a world where you can share your joys and concerns, knowing that others will listen and support you.

Learning how to share your feelings isn't just about vulnerability; it's about fostering healthier connections with those around you. So, get ready to explore the steps that will help you open up about your emotions without feeling vulnerable.

Step 1: Identify Your Emotions

capitalize

- Recognize and label the emotions you're feeling in a specific situation. *(refer to the appendix for an emotions list)*

Step 2: Use "I" Statements for Emotions

- Express your emotions using "I" statements to clearly convey how you feel without blaming or accusing others.

Step 3: Vulnerability and Empathy

- Be open about your feelings and empathize with others' perspectives and emotions during the conversation.

Sample Scenarios

1. Friend's Behavior

- Step 1: Recognize that you're feeling disappointed and frustrated about your friend's cancellations.

- Step 2: Instead of saying, "You always cancel on me," say, "I've been feeling disappointed and frustrated because our plans keep getting canceled."

- Step 3: Be open about your feelings, and when your friend responds, try to understand their perspective and feelings as well.

2. Sibling's Behavior

- Step 1: Recognize that you're feeling annoyed and frustrated about your sibling borrowing your things without permission.

- Step 2: Instead of saying, "You should stop taking my stuff," say, "I've been feeling annoyed and frustrated because my things are borrowed without asking."

- Step 3: Be open about your feelings, and if your sibling responds, try to understand their perspective and feelings as well.

3. Team Project Challenges

- Step 1: Recognize that you're feeling stressed and overwhelmed due to the project challenges.

- Step 2: Instead of saying, "This project is a disaster," say, "I've been feeling stressed and overwhelmed because of the challenges we're facing in the project."

- Step 3: Be open about your feelings, and when your team members respond, try to understand their perspectives and feelings as well.

Assertive Requests: The Art of Getting What You Need

Assertive requests are like the secret sauce to getting your needs met while maintaining healthy relationships. In this section, we're going to unveil the power of making requests assertively and how it can level up your interactions.

Imagine a world where you can ask for what you need with confidence, clarity, and respect. It's a world where others appreciate your straightforwardness and are more willing to support you.

Assertive requests aren't about demanding or manipulating; they're about clear and respectful communication. Whether you're asking for help, expressing your preferences, or setting boundaries, learning this skill will empower you to navigate your relationships with finesse.

Now, let's explore the steps to master the art of making assertive requests and getting what you need while strengthening your connections with others.

Step 1: Identify Your Needs

- Recognize and define what you need or want in a specific situation.

Step 2: Use Clear and Direct Language

- Clearly and directly communicate your request using polite language.

Step 3: Respectful Communication

- Make your request respectfully, and express gratitude when others respond positively.

Sample Scenarios

1. Homework Help

- Step 1: Recognize that you need help understanding a particular homework assignment.

- Step 2: Instead of saying, "Can you explain this to me?" say, "Could you please help me understand how to solve this math problem?"

- Step 3: Make your request politely, and express gratitude when your classmate offers assistance.

2. Chores at Home

- Step 1: Recognize that you need your sibling's assistance with chores to save time.

- Step 2: Instead of saying, "Can you do some chores?" say, "Could you please help with the dishes and vacuuming today? I have a lot on my plate."

- Step 3: Make your request respectfully

Overcoming Barriers to Assertiveness: Crushing Common Obstacles

Assertiveness isn't always a walk in the park. Sometimes, you'll face obstacles that try to block your path. But don't worry, we've got strategies to help you overcome them.

1. Fear of Rejection

The fear of rejection can be a powerful barrier to assertiveness. It's the worry that if you express your thoughts, feelings, or needs, others might not like you or respond negatively. Overcoming this fear is essential for confident communication.

Steps:

1. Self-Affirmation: Remind yourself of your worth and value. Your opinions and needs matter.

2. Reframe Rejection: Realize that rejection doesn't define your entire worth or your ability to assert yourself.

3. Practice with Safe Scenarios: Start with low-stakes situations to build confidence in your assertiveness.

Sample Scenarios

- ***Scenario 1:*** *Your best friend suggests going to a different restaurant for dinner, but you prefer your favorite place. You say, "I really enjoy our favorite spot. How about we go there tonight?"*

- ***Scenario 2:*** *Your younger sibling wants to play with your toys, but you're worried they might break them. You say, "I'd love to play together, but let's choose toys that we both can enjoy safely."*

- ***Scenario 3:*** *Your classmate asks if you want to join their study group, but you already have other plans. You say, "Thanks for the invite! I've got some commitments tonight, but I'd love to join next time."*

2. Guilt and People-Pleasing

Feeling guilty for asserting yourself or constantly trying to please others can hinder assertiveness. It's time to prioritize your needs and well-being while maintaining healthy relationships.

Steps:

1. Recognize Your Needs: Acknowledge that your needs are valid and deserve consideration.

2. Set Healthy Boundaries: Clearly define your boundaries and communicate them assertively.

3. Practice Self-Compassion: Be kind to yourself and understand that it's okay to prioritize your well-being.

Sample Scenarios

- ***Scenario 1:*** *Your friend keeps borrowing your notes without asking, and it's affecting your own studying. You say, "I'm happy to help, but I need to use my notes for my own studying. Let's find another solution."*

- ***Scenario 2:*** *Your cousin frequently asks you for rides to various places, making you feel overwhelmed. You say, "I want to help, but it's becoming a bit much for me to manage. Let's discuss a more balanced arrangement."*

- ***Scenario 3:*** *Your teammate wants you to take on extra work for a group project, but you're already handling your fair share. You say, "I'm doing my part, and I'd appreciate it if we could distribute the workload more evenly."*

3. Conflict Anxiety

Many people fear conflict and the tension it brings. This anxiety can lead to avoiding necessary conversations and compromise assertiveness. Learning to handle conflicts assertively is a valuable skill.

Steps:

1. Preparation: Plan what you want to say and the desired outcome of the conversation.

2. Active Listening: Listen attentively to the other person's perspective, showing empathy and understanding.

3. Use "I" Statements: Express your thoughts and feelings using "I" statements to avoid blame and accusations.

Sample Scenarios

- *Scenario 1:* Your friend borrowed your laptop without asking, and it got damaged. You say, "I noticed my laptop was damaged after you used it. Can we talk about how to address this situation?"

- *Scenario 2:* Your roommate constantly plays loud music late at night, making it hard for you to sleep. You say, "I've had trouble sleeping due to the loud music. Can we find a compromise that works for both of us?"

- *Scenario 3:* Your family member borrowed your clothes without permission, and they got stained. You say, "I noticed my clothes were stained after they were borrowed. Can we talk about how to handle this?"

Assertiveness Training Worksheet

Assertiveness Skills: The Art of Speaking Your Truth

1. Expressing Thoughts

Describe a recent situation where you had thoughts or opinions but didn't express them assertively.

Sample Response: *"I was in a group project, and I had ideas for our presentation, but I didn't speak up because I was afraid others wouldn't agree."*

How could you have expressed your thoughts more assertively in that situation?

Sample Response: *"I could have said, 'I have some ideas for our presentation that I think could improve it. Can we discuss them?'"*

2. Sharing Feelings

Think of a time when you felt a strong emotion but didn't express it assertively. Describe the situation and your feelings.

Sample Response: *"I was upset when my friend canceled our plans last minute without any explanation."*

How might you have shared your feelings assertively in that situation?

Sample Response: *"I could have said, 'I feel disappointed and a bit hurt when plans change last minute without notice. Can we try to avoid this in the future?'"*

3. Assertive Requests

Recall an instance when you needed something from someone but didn't make an assertive request. What was the situation?

Sample Response: *"I needed my coworker to complete their part of a project on time, but I didn't ask them directly."*

How could you have made an assertive request in that situation?

Sample Response: *"I could have said, 'I need your part of the project by Friday to meet our deadline. Can you please ensure it's done by then?'"*

Overcoming Barriers to Assertiveness: Crushing Common Obstacles

5. Fear of Rejection

Have you ever avoided expressing yourself because you were afraid of someone's reaction or rejection? Describe the situation.

Sample Response: *"I didn't speak up in a group discussion because I was afraid my idea might be rejected, and others wouldn't like it."*

How can you overcome the fear of rejection in similar situations?

Sample Response: *"I can remind myself that it's okay if not everyone agrees with me. I can focus on sharing my ideas confidently."*

6. Guilt and People-Pleasing:

Share a situation where you felt guilty for asserting yourself or tried to please someone at the expense of your needs.

Sample Response: *"I agreed to take on extra responsibilities at work even though I was already overloaded because I didn't want to disappoint my boss."*

What strategies can you use to avoid feeling guilty or prioritize your needs in the future?

Sample Response: *"I can set clear boundaries and communicate my workload more effectively to my boss to prevent overloading myself."*

7. Conflict Anxiety:

Recall a time when you avoided a necessary conflict or difficult conversation due to anxiety. Describe the situation.

Sample Response: *"I didn't address a disagreement with my friend because I was afraid it would turn into an argument."*

How can you better handle conflicts assertively while managing anxiety?

Sample Response: *"I can prepare for the conversation, actively listen to my friend's perspective, and use 'I' statements to express my feelings calmly."*

Use this worksheet to practice assertiveness skills and overcome common barriers in various aspects of your life. Remember that assertiveness is a valuable tool for effective communication and building healthier relationships.

Song Recommendation: "Lean on Me" by Bill Withers

Section 3: Creating a Support System (ACT): Building Your Squad

In the world of Acceptance and Commitment Therapy (ACT), building a support system emerges as the ultimate sidekick to our superhero mindset. Think of it as a trusty ally that perfectly aligns with the ACT principle of "Commitment." Creating a support system is like leveling up your commitment to personal growth and well-being. It's about recognizing that you don't have to face life's challenges solo; instead, you team up with friends, family, or anyone who's got your back.

Here's why building this network is essential:

1. Strength in Connections

- Life can throw curveballs, and it's easier to face them with others by your side. Your support network provides a safety net of people you can lean on when times get tough.

Sample Scenario: *You're dealing with a challenging personal situation, and you turn to your close friend who has faced a similar issue before. They offer advice and emotional support, making you feel less alone in your struggles.*

2. Emotional Support

- Everyone has moments when they doubt themselves or feel overwhelmed. Your support system offers emotional backup, providing encouragement, a listening ear, and a reminder of your strengths.

Sample Scenario: You're pursuing a new hobby that's outside your comfort zone, and you're feeling anxious. Your support network includes a mentor who's been through the same journey. They share their experiences and offer words of encouragement, boosting your confidence.

3. Accountability and Motivation

- Your support network keeps you on track with your goals and dreams. They hold you accountable for your actions, provide constructive feedback, and motivate you to keep pushing forward.

Sample Scenario: You have a long-term project to complete, and your support network includes a study group. They meet regularly, review each other's progress, and provide motivation to stay focused and productive.

Building your support system isn't just about having people around; it's about nurturing meaningful connections with those who genuinely care about your growth and well-being.

Identifying Potential Support Sources: Building Your Dream Team

In this section, we're going to help you identify the people or groups who can become your go-to crew for support. Think of it as curating your dream team of allies who will have your back along the way.

Here's how to go about it:

1. Checking Out Your Current Squad

- Take a look at your current friendships and family connections. Figure out those who've always had your back, listened without judgment, and cheered you on.

Sample Scenario: You've got this buddy, Alex, who's always there when you need to talk things out. They're super understanding and give awesome advice, making them a top candidate for your support squad.

2. Scoping Out New BFFs

- Sometimes, you can expand your crew by making new pals. Seek out mentors, fellow peeps with similar interests, or squads that vibe with your values and goals.

Sample Scenario: You joined a cool club at school that's all about your favorite hobby. In the group, you've clicked with a wise mentor who knows the ropes and can guide you—perfect support squad material!

3. Finding Kindred Spirits

- Hunt down individuals or groups who share your vibes, beliefs, or dreams. When you're on the same wavelength, it's easier to build tight-knit bonds.

Sample Scenario : You're all about saving the planet, and you've stumbled upon a local eco-warrior group. These peeps are all about green living, just like you, making them potential support squad material.

Remember, it's not about having a massive entourage; it's about having a squad that's got your back and genuinely cares about your journey. They're the ones who'll ride with you through thick and thin, offering guidance and support.

Building and Maintaining Relationships: Nurturing Your Dream Team

Now, let's dive into some strategies to nurture and keep your essential relationships strong. Your squad is there for the long haul, so it's time to make sure those connections thrive.

Here's the game plan:

1. Cultivating Connection

- Building strong relationships starts with investing time and effort in them. Show your peeps that you care about them and value their presence.

Sample Scenario: You regularly catch up with your bestie, Mark, over video calls even though you live in different cities. Your effort to maintain the connection strengthens your friendship.

2. Effective Communication

- Communication is the secret sauce for any healthy relationship. Keep those lines of communication open and honest.

Sample Scenario: You and your sibling, Alex, had a little disagreement. You both talked it out, listened to each other, and found a solution that works for both of you.

3. Offering Support

- Being there for your squad when they need you is crucial. Whether it's celebrating their wins or lending a helping hand during tough times, your support means the world.

Sample Scenario: Your friend, Jess, is going through a challenging phase. You check in on her regularly, offer a listening ear, and help her find resources for support.

Remember, relationships take effort and care. By cultivating connection, communicating effectively, and offering support, you'll not only build strong bonds but also create a squad that's there for you, no matter what. Let's keep these good vibes rolling as we explore more ways to enhance your relationships and live your best life.

Building Your Dream Team: Master Worksheet

It's time to level up your support network and relationships. This worksheet is your guide to creating a dream team of allies who have your back and help you stay true to your values and goals. Let's dive in!

Recognizing the Importance of Support

1. Values Check-In

List three values that are super important to you.

Sample Response: Honesty, kindness, creativity.

> 1.
> 2.
> 3.

2. Why Support Matters

Write a paragraph explaining why having a support system aligns with your personal values. How can they help you stay true to what matters most to you?

Sample Response: Having a support system is crucial because my values include kindness and personal growth. When I surround myself with supportive friends and family, it's easier to be kind to others and myself. They motivate me to work on self-improvement, which aligns with my value of personal growth.

Identifying Potential Support Sources

3. Dream Team Assemble

List at least five people or groups who could be part of your support network. These could be friends, family members, teachers, clubs, or online communities.

Sample Response:

Family: Mom, Dad, Grandma; Friends: Sarah, Alex, Jess; School: Art Club, Mr. Johnson (teacher)

4. Choose Wisely

Circle the three potential support sources you feel most comfortable reaching out to. Why did you choose them?

Sample Response: I chose my best friend, Sarah, because she's always been there for me, my sister, because we can talk about anything, and my school's art club because I feel a sense of belonging there.

Building and Maintaining Relationships

5. Cultivating Connection

Think of a family member (F), friend (Fr), or school relationship (S). How can you invest time and effort in nurturing your relationship with them? Describe at least one action you can take for each category.

Sample Response:

(F) I can spend quality time with my dad by going for a bike ride together this weekend.

(Fr) I can support my friend Jess by listening to her when she needs to talk and sending her positive messages.

(S) I can improve my school relationship with Mr. Johnson by attending his extra help sessions and actively participating in class.

6. Effective Communication

Imagine a recent misunderstanding with someone close to you (family, friend, or school). How could you have communicated more effectively to avoid or resolve the conflict? Describe the improved communication approach for each category.

Sample Response:

(F) My mom and I had a disagreement about chores. I could have calmly explained my perspective and listened to hers.

(Fr) I had a misunderstanding with my friend Alex. I could have actively listened to their point of view without interrupting.

(S) I had a conflict with a classmate. I could have asked for clarification on their perspective before jumping to conclusions.

7. Offering Support

Name a family member (F), friend (Fr), or school contact (S) who might need support right now. How can you be there for them during this time? List at least two ways you can provide support for each category.

Sample Response:

(F) My grandma could use some company. I can call her regularly and visit her.

(Fr) My friend Sarah is going through a tough time. I can check in on her regularly and offer a listening ear.

(S) A classmate is struggling with a project. I can offer to study together and share helpful resources.

Remember, superstar, building and maintaining meaningful relationships takes effort and care. By working on these aspects, you're on your way to creating a dream team that's there for you, no matter what life throws your way. Keep rocking those connection!

Song Recommendation: "Count On Me" by Bruno Mars

Conclusion

Review of Key Concepts

In this chapter, we've delved into a world of valuable skills and insights that can transform the way you navigate relationships and interactions with others. Let's take a moment to recap the essential concepts you've explored.

Interpersonal Effectiveness

You've gained an understanding of the importance of interpersonal skills, objective effectiveness in setting and achieving goals, strategies for improving relationships, and maintaining self-respect in your interactions. These skills are fundamental for building and nurturing healthy connections with others.

Assertiveness Training

You've dived into the world of assertiveness, learning how to express your thoughts, feelings, and needs with confidence. Assertiveness is a key component of effective communication and plays a vital role in your relationships.

Creating a Support System

You've explored the significance of having a support network, identifying potential sources of support, communicating your needs and boundaries effectively, and building and maintaining relationships with individuals who form your "dream team."

6

WHO AM I?

Introduction

Welcome to Chapter 6 of *Therapy Vibes*. In this chapter, we're embarking on a journey of self-discovery and personal growth. Think of this chapter as a treasure hunt within yourself, where you'll uncover the gems that make you unique and learn how to embrace and celebrate your true self.

Section 1: Exploring Your Self-Identity

Understanding Self-Identity

Defining Self-Identity

Imagine you're a teenager who's super into music, especially playing the guitar. It's not just a hobby; it's a big part of who you are. Your self-identity is like a mixtape of what makes you, well, you. It's all about what you're into, what you believe, and how you see yourself.

- **Getting what self-identity is:** Self-identity is like your personal playlist. It's everything that makes you unique, from your favorite bands and beliefs to your talents and what you've been through.
- **Different parts of self-identity:** Your self-identity isn't just one song; it's an entire album with different tracks. This includes your values, the stuff you believe in, your interests, talents, experiences, and even where your family comes from. All these things make up your self-identity.
- **It's not set in stone:** Just like your music tastes can change, your self-identity can too. As you grow, learn, and experience new things, your self-identity can evolve and grow with you.

- **Why self-identity matters:** Think of your self-identity as your personal GPS. It helps you figure out where you want to go and how to get there. When you know who you are and what you stand for, you can make choices that match your true self.

- **Feeling good all-around:** Living in harmony with your self-identity can lead to feeling pretty awesome. It's like finding the perfect rhythm in your life. When you're true to yourself, you're more likely to feel happy and satisfied.

By being aware of your self-identity, you're basically becoming a detective of your own awesomeness. It helps you understand how you think, feel, and act in different situations (CBT), and how you can use it to your advantage. Embrace your unique self-identity, and it'll be your guiding star on this journey of self-discovery and personal growth.

What Happens Without a Stable Identity?

Imagine this: You're at a party, and people keep asking you what kind of music you like, but you're not sure. You start with hip-hop because your friend likes it, but then someone mentions classical, and you think, "Maybe I like that too." You end up feeling awkward and unsure about your own preferences.

Without a stable self-identity, it's like being at that party all the time. You might :

- Struggle with making choices because you're not sure what you really want.

- Feel like you're putting on different masks in different situations to fit in.

- Have a hard time explaining who you are or what you stand for to others.

- Experience a sense of confusion or dissatisfaction in your life because it's like trying to solve a puzzle with missing pieces.

Challenging and Reframing Negative Beliefs About Yourself

In this section, we'll delve into the common negative beliefs and self-critical thoughts that many of us carry. These beliefs can hold us back, diminish our self-esteem, and hinder personal growth. It's essential to recognize these beliefs to begin the process of transforming them. Some common self-limiting beliefs include:

- "I'm not good enough."

- "I always mess things up."

- "Nobody likes me."

- "I'll never succeed."

Identifying these beliefs is the first step towards challenging and changing them.

: Chapter 3 Vibes

Cognitive Restructuring for Self-Identity: Applying What You Learned in Chapter 3

In this section, we're taking the principles of cognitive restructuring that you learned in Chapter 3 and applying them specifically to your self-identity. These techniques will help you address and reframe negative thoughts related to how you perceive yourself.

Step 1: Identifying Negative Self-Identity Thoughts

- You've already learned about identifying negative thoughts in Chapter 3. Now, let's focus on recognizing negative thoughts related to your self-identity.

- These thoughts might sound like, "I'm not good enough," "I'll never fit in," or "I'm always a failure."

Step 2: Evaluating Your Self-Identity Thoughts

- Remember the importance of evaluating the accuracy of your thoughts. Just like in Chapter 3, you'll question the validity of these self-identity thoughts.

- For example, if you think, "I'll never fit in," ask yourself if there are times when you did feel like you belonged.

Step 3: Reframing Your Self-Identity Thoughts

- Building on what you learned about cognitive restructuring, replace negative self-identity thoughts with more balanced and positive ones.

- Instead of saying, "I'm not good enough," try thinking, "I have strengths and qualities that make me unique."

Step 4: Cultivating Positive Self-Talk

- Continue practicing positive self-talk, which you started exploring in Chapter 3. Treat yourself with kindness and compassion, just as you would a good friend.

- If you make a mistake, remind yourself, "It's okay; everyone makes mistakes, and I can learn from this."

Step 5: Keeping a Self-Identity Journal

- Remember the concept of keeping a journal to track your thoughts and progress. Document negative self-identity thoughts, the situations that trigger them, and your feelings.

- Then, record the new, balanced thoughts you replace them with. This journal will help you see how you're applying cognitive restructuring to self-identity.

Here are three sample scenarios to demonstrate how to apply cognitive restructuring to self-identity thoughts:

Scenario 1: Fear of Not Being Good Enough

1. Negative Self-Identity Thought: "I'm not good enough to audition for the school play. Everyone else is so talented, and I'll just embarrass myself."

2. Challenging the Thought

- Ask yourself, "Is this thought based on facts, or am I making assumptions?"

- Recall times when you've practiced and improved your acting skills. Remind yourself of your dedication and hard work.

3. Reframed Self-Identity Thought: "I've put in effort to improve my acting skills, and I have my unique interpretation to bring to the audition. It's natural to feel nervous, but I'm capable of giving it my best shot."

italicize?

Scenario 2: Feeling Like an Outsider

1. Negative Self-Identity Thought: "I'm always the outsider in social situations. Nobody really wants to be my friend."

2. Challenging the Thought

- Ask yourself, "Is this thought accurate, or am I assuming the worst?"

- Recall moments when you've connected with others and made friends. Recognize that feeling like an outsider occasionally is normal.

3. Reframed Self-Identity Thought: "While I may have felt like an outsider at times, I've also had moments of connection and friendship. It's okay to have moments of insecurity, but I'm open to new connections and building relationships."

Scenario 3: Feeling Overwhelmed by Expectations

1. Negative Self-Identity Thought: "I'll never meet the expectations my family has for me. They want me to be perfect, and I'm just not."

2. Challenging the Thought

- Ask yourself, "Are these expectations truly realistic, or am I putting too much pressure on myself?"

- Reflect on your achievements and acknowledge that perfection is unattainable. Everyone makes mistakes and faces challenges.

3. Reframed Self-Identity Thought: "While I may not meet every expectation, I've accomplished things I'm proud of. It's important to strive for my own goals and well-being, rather than trying to be perfect according to someone else's standards."

These sample scenarios illustrate how to identify, challenge, and reframe negative self-identity thoughts using cognitive restructuring techniques. By applying these steps, you can build a more positive and realistic self-identity that reflects your strengths, potential, and self-worth.

Building a More Positive Self-narrative

Developing a positive self-narrative is crucial for improving self-esteem and self-identity. We'll introduce concepts related to self-compassion and self-acceptance. You'll learn how to cultivate a kinder and more accepting inner dialogue, counteracting the negativity that may have plagued your self-perception.

When you spot those sneaky thoughts holding you back, and you learn how to flip the script using mind ninja moves, and you start being your own biggest cheerleader, you're basically turning your self-talk into a hype squad that's got your back. This is your secret weapon for a healthier and way more awesome self-identity.

It's totally normal to have those moments where you doubt yourself, but guess what? You've got the power to change the game and build a self-identity that's all about celebrating the real you.

Section 2: Practicing Self-Compassion

Understanding Self-Compassion

Self-compassion is like giving yourself a warm hug when you're feeling down. It's all about treating yourself with kindness and understanding, just as you would a close friend.

Think of it as a gentle and caring attitude towards yourself, especially when you make mistakes or face difficulties.

Benefits of Self-Compassion

- Self-compassion is a key component of Dialectical Behavior Therapy (DBT), which helps individuals manage their emotions and improve relationships.

- It boosts your self-esteem and self-identity, making you feel more confident and accepting of who you are.

- Self-compassion reduces self-criticism and negative self-talk, leading to less stress and anxiety, which are core elements of DBT.

Practical Self-Compassion Exercises

Exercise 1: Self-Compassionate Letter

Step 1: Write a Letter to Yourself

- Find a quiet and comfortable space where you can focus without distractions. It could be at a desk, on your bed, or in a cozy corner.

- Take out a notebook, journal, or a sheet of paper and begin by addressing the letter to yourself. You can start with "Dear [Your Name]."

Step 2: Offer Encouragement and Support

- In your letter, start by offering yourself words of encouragement and support. Imagine you're writing to a dear friend who's going through a tough time.

- Acknowledge any challenges you're currently facing or any difficult emotions you're experiencing. Express empathy for yourself.

Step 3: Reflect and Validate

- Reflect on specific situations or difficulties that you've encountered recently or in the past. This could be related to school, relationships, personal goals, or anything else that has been on your mind.

- Write about these experiences in a way that validates your feelings and experiences without judgment. Remember that it's okay to feel the way you do.

Step 4: Self-Compassionate Affirmations

- Include self-compassionate affirmations in your letter. These are positive and comforting statements that can counteract self-criticism.

- For example, you can write phrases like:
  - "You are worthy of love and acceptance just as you are."
  - "Mistakes are a part of growth, and I'm here to support you through them."
  - "I believe in your abilities and your resilience."

Sample Letter

Imagine you recently experienced a setback in a personal project, and you're feeling disappointed and self-critical. Here's how you can structure your self-compassionate letter:

"Dear [Your Name],

I want you to know that I understand how you're feeling right now. It's tough when things don't go as planned, and it's okay to be disappointed. Remember, setbacks are a part of life, and they don't define your worth.

I admire your determination and the effort you put into your project. Even though it didn't turn out the way you hoped, it's a valuable learning experience. You have the strength to bounce back and continue moving forward.

Please be kind to yourself during this time. Treat yourself with the same kindness and understanding that you would offer to a close friend. You deserve it.

With love and understanding,

[Your Name]"

Writing a self-compassionate letter can be a powerful way to practice self-kindness and improve your self-identity. It's a reminder that you are your own best friend and supporter, and you can offer yourself the same comfort and encouragement that you would offer to someone you care about.

Exercise 2: Positive Self-Affirmations (Review of Chapter 4)

Step 1: Create Your Affirmations

- Find a quiet and comfortable space where you can focus on creating positive self-affirmations.

- Take out a notebook, journal, or a digital document where you can write down your affirmations.

Step 2: Write Positive Statements About Yourself

- Start by writing down positive statements or affirmations about yourself. These should be statements that boost your self-identity and self-worth.

- You can structure them as "I am..." statements. For example:

  - "I am capable of achieving my goals."

  - "I am worthy of love and respect."

  - "I am resilient and can overcome challenges."

Step 3: Repeat Daily

- Make it a daily practice to repeat these affirmations to yourself. You can do this in the morning, before bedtime, or whenever you need a confidence boost.

- You can say these affirmations aloud or silently in your mind, whichever feels most comfortable to you.

Sample Scenario

Imagine you often doubt your abilities, and self-doubt creeps in before a big presentation.

Positive Self-Affirmation Response:

1. Find a quiet moment to sit or stand comfortably.
2. Begin by reciting your positive self-affirmations. For instance, say to yourself:

   - *"I am well-prepared for this presentation."*

   - *"I have valuable insights to share with my audience."*

   - *"I can confidently present my ideas and make a positive impact."*

Practicing positive self-affirmations is a powerful way to reshape your self-identity and boost your self-esteem.

Exercise 3: Inner Critic vs. Inner Friend

Step 1: Visualize the Conversation

- Find a comfortable and quiet space where you can visualize this inner dialogue without distractions.

- Close your eyes and take a few deep breaths to center yourself.

Step 2: Imagine the Conversation

- In your mind, imagine a conversation taking place between two distinct voices within you: your inner critic and your inner friend.

- Visualize your inner critic as the voice that tends to be self-critical, negative, or judgmental. This is the voice that often undermines your self-identity.

- Your inner friend is the compassionate and supportive voice within you. It's the voice that offers comfort, understanding, and kindness.

Step 3: Challenge Negative Thoughts

As you imagine this conversation unfolding, let your inner friend challenge the negative thoughts brought up by your inner critic. Your inner friend should provide counterarguments and self-compassionate responses.

Sample Scenario

Your inner critic is saying, "You'll never make any friends; you're too awkward."

Inner Critic vs. Inner Friend Response:

1. Close your eyes and visualize the inner critic speaking these words.

2. Imagine your inner friend stepping in and saying, "Awkward moments happen to everyone, and they don't define your ability to make friends. You have unique qualities that people appreciate."

3. Continue the conversation in your mind, with your inner friend offering more reassuring and self-compassionate responses to counteract the negativity of your inner critic.

Practicing the inner critic vs. inner friend exercise can help you become more aware of your self-talk and shift towards a more self-compassionate and positive self-identity.

Exercise 4: Self-Compassionate Breathing

Step 1: Find a Calm Space

- Seek a quiet and peaceful space where you can comfortably practice self-compassionate breathing.

- It can be a chair, a cushion, or any place where you feel relaxed.

Step 2: Deep Breathing Technique

Begin by practicing deep and calming breaths. Here's a step-by-step guide:

1. Inhale slowly and deeply through your nose, counting to four. Feel your lungs fill with air.

2. Hold your breath for a moment at the top of your inhale.

3. Exhale slowly and fully through your mouth or nose, also counting to four. Imagine releasing tension and self-judgment with each exhale.

4. Pause for a moment at the bottom of your exhale.

Step 3: Visualize Self-Compassion

As you continue deep breathing, visualize the following:

Inhale self-compassion, understanding, and kindness with each breath. Imagine these qualities as a soothing, warm light entering your body.

Feel a sense of calm and self-acceptance washing over you with every exhale. Imagine it as a cleansing release of self-judgment and negativity.

Sample Scenario

You're feeling overwhelmed by self-criticism after receiving a less-than-perfect grade on a test.

Self-Compassionate Breathing Response:

1. Find a quiet and comfortable space to sit or lie down.

2. Begin practicing deep and calming breaths. Inhale slowly for a count of four, hold for a moment, and exhale for a count of four.

3. As you continue breathing, visualize inhaling self-compassion, understanding, and kindness. Imagine these qualities as a soothing, warm light filling your entire being.

4. With each exhale, let go of self-judgment and negativity. Visualize them leaving your body, making space for self-acceptance and inner calm.

seems lowey?

Section 3: Defining Your Personal Values

In this section, we delve into the profound impact of personal values on shaping your life and self-identity. Understanding your values is a crucial aspect of Acceptance and Commitment Therapy (ACT) and self-discovery.

In Chapter 3, we touched on identifying and aligning with your values. Now, we're taking a deeper dive into this essential aspect of personal growth. By discovering, clarifying, and prioritizing your values, you'll gain greater insight into who you are, what matters most to you, and how to live a fulfilling life that aligns with your authentic self.

Understanding the Profound Role of Personal Values

Imagine values as the roots of a tree. Just like the roots provide stability and nourishment to the tree, your values provide stability and purpose to your life. Values are practical guides that influence your everyday decisions and actions. Your values shape the choices you make in various aspects of your life, from relationships and career to personal goals and hobbies.

For example, if one of your core values is compassion, you're more likely to engage in acts of kindness and empathy in your interactions with others. If you highly value creativity, you'll be drawn to artistic pursuits and innovative thinking.

Exploring the Connection Between Values and Overall Well-Being

The alignment between your values and your life choices has a profound impact on your overall well-being. When you live in harmony with your values, you experience a sense of fulfillment, purpose, and authenticity. This alignment enhances your self-identity, making you feel more grounded and connected to your true self.

On the other hand, when you neglect or compromise your values, you may experience feelings of dissonance, frustration, and dissatisfaction. This misalignment can erode your self-identity and lead to a sense of emptiness or inner conflict.

Exploring Your Core Values and Self-Identity Worksheet

Instructions: In this worksheet, we will dive deeper into your core values and their connection to your self-identity. Refer to the values you identified in Chapter 3 as a starting point, and let's explore how these values shape who you are.

Part 1: Reviewing Your Core Values (Refer to Chapter 3)

1. List the core values you identified in Chapter 3.

Value 1: _____[Sample Response: Creativity]

Value 2: _____[Sample Response: Compassion]

Value 3: _____[Sample Response: Integrity]

2. Reflect on why these values resonate with you. What is it about each value that makes it important to you? Write a brief description for each.

Sample responses:

Value 1 (Creativity): *[Sample Response: Creativity resonates with me because it allows me to express myself and find unique solutions to problems. It brings joy and fulfillment to my life.]*

Value 2 (Compassion): *[Sample Response: Compassion is important to me because it reminds me to be kind and understanding towards others, fostering positive relationships and empathy.]*

Value 3 (Integrity): *[Sample Response: Integrity is crucial as it is the foundation of my self-respect. It ensures I stay true to my principles and morals.]*

Part 2: Connecting Values to Self-Identity

3. Choose one of your core values from the list above.

4. Reflect on how this value influences your self-identity. How does it shape your beliefs, decisions, and actions? Write about specific moments or experiences where this value played a significant role in defining who you are.

Sample Responses:

Value Selected (Creativity): *Creativity is at the heart of my self-identity. It molds my beliefs by encouraging me to see the world as a canvas for self-expression and problem-solving. For instance, I recall a time when our school organized an art competition. I poured my heart into creating a unique and imaginative piece of art. This experience highlighted that my self-identity thrives on innovation and artistic expression.*

Value Selected (Compassion): *Compassion is a fundamental part of my self-identity. It guides my beliefs by reminding me to see the world through a lens of kindness and empathy. For example, I remember a time when a new student joined our school, and many kids were making fun of them. My value of compassion kicked in, and I decided to befriend the new student, offering support and friendship. This experience showed me that my self-identity is rooted in being there for others and promoting positivity.*

Value Selected (Integrity): *[Sample Response: Integrity deeply influences my self-identity. It guides me to be honest and principled in everything I do. For instance, I remember a situation where I found a wallet with money in it. My value of integrity led me to return it to the owner, even though I could have kept the money. This experience reinforced that my self-identity is closely tied to honesty and doing what's right.]*

5. Now, think about a time when you acted in a way that was not aligned with this value. How did it make you feel? What did you learn from that experience about the importance of staying true to your values?

Sample Responses:

Situation where I didn't align with my value (Creativity): *There was an instance when I followed a conventional approach to a school project because I thought it would be easier and more acceptable. It left me feeling uninspired and unfulfilled. I realized that straying from my core value of creativity left me disconnected from my true self. It taught me that embracing creativity is vital for my self-identity and personal satisfaction.*

Situation where I didn't align with my value (Compassion): *There was a situation where I joined in with some friends who were teasing a classmate. I felt terrible afterward because it went against my core value of compassion. It made me realize that compromising on my values to fit in with others only leads to regret and that staying true to my value of compassion is crucial for my self-identity and overall well-being.*

Situation where I didn't align with my value (Integrity): *[Sample Response: There was a time when I copied someone else's homework out of fear of getting a low grade. It made me feel guilty and ashamed because it went against my core value of integrity. This experience taught me that compromising on my values erodes my self-identity and damages my self-esteem.]*

Part 3: Exploring the Connection

6. Analyze the relationship between your core values and your self-identity. How do your values reflect who you are? How does living in alignment with your values contribute to a more authentic self-identity?

Sample Responses:

Connection between my values and self-identity (Creativity): *My values and self-identity are intertwined when it comes to creativity. Creativity is a reflection of my identity, emphasizing the importance of self-expression and innovative thinking. When I create or think outside the box, I feel more genuine and connected to my true self. It's like my way of showing the world who I am and what I believe in.*

Connection between my values and self-identity (Compassion): *Compassion is like the compass of my self-identity. It points me toward kindness, empathy, and building meaningful connections with others. When I act with compassion, I genuinely feel like I'm being the best version of myself. It's a reminder that being there for others and spreading positivity is a big part of who I am.*

Connection between my values and self-identity (Integrity): *Integrity is the cornerstone of my self-identity. It defines me as an honest and principled person. When I act with integrity, I feel a deep sense of authenticity and self-respect. It's a reminder that staying true to my values is at the core of who I am.*

7. What steps can you take to ensure that your actions and choices continue to align with your core values? How can this support your self-identity and personal growth?

Sample Responses:

Steps to align with my values and support self-identity (Creativity): *To stay true to my value of creativity, I'll make time for creative pursuits regularly. Whether it's painting, writing, or problem-solving in unique ways, I'll keep nurturing my creative side. This will not only reinforce my self-identity but also help me grow personally by expanding my creative skills and perspectives.*

Steps to align with my values and support self-identity (Compassion): *To stay aligned with my value of compassion, I'll actively seek opportunities to help others and show kindness. Whether it's volunteering, lending a listening ear, or practicing empathy in daily life, these actions will reinforce my self-identity as a compassionate person and foster personal growth through deeper connections with others.*

Steps to align with my values and support self-identity (Integrity): *To maintain my integrity, I'll consistently make choices that prioritize honesty and moral principles. This includes admitting my mistakes and taking responsibility for my actions. These steps will not only strengthen my self-identity as a person of integrity but also contribute to personal growth by fostering a strong sense of self-respect and trustworthiness.*

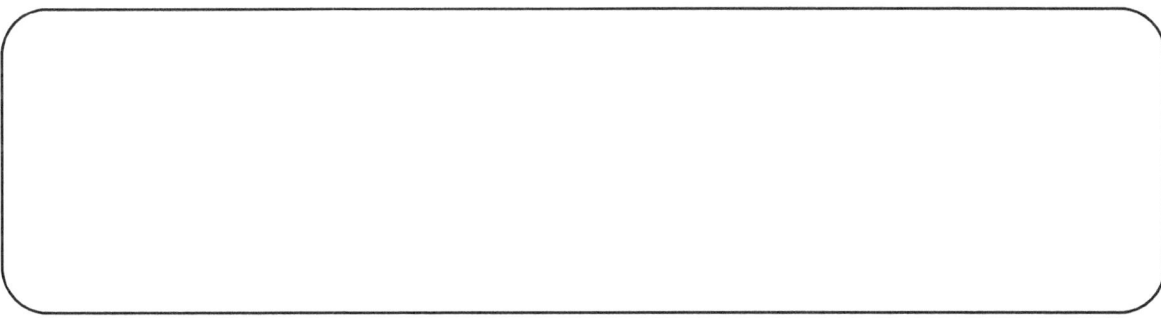

By exploring the connection between your core values and self-identity, you're taking a crucial step in understanding how these values shape your authentic self. Use this worksheet as a tool to strengthen the alignment between your values and who you are, ultimately leading to a more fulfilling and genuine life.

Overcoming Obstacles to Living Authentically

1. Fear of Judgment

The fear of being judged or criticized for your values can be paralyzing. It might lead you to hide your true self or make choices that don't align with your values just to avoid negative opinions.

Example: Let's say your core value is "environmental sustainability," and you choose to bring a reusable water bottle to school even though some classmates tease you for it. Overcoming this fear involves reminding yourself that you're honoring a value that matters to you and focusing on self-acceptance rather than seeking approval from others.

2. Lack of Confidence

A lack of confidence can hold you back from expressing your authentic self and making value-aligned choices. It often stems from self-doubt and the belief that you're not capable of living according to your values.

Example: Suppose you value "leadership" but doubt your ability to lead a school club. Overcoming this obstacle means taking small steps to build confidence, such as volunteering for a leadership role within your comfort zone and gradually expanding your responsibilities.

3. External Expectations

External expectations from society, family, or cultural norms can sometimes clash with your values. It's essential to navigate these expectations while staying true to your authentic self.

Example: If your family expects you to pursue a specific career that doesn't align with your values, communication is key. You can express your values and explain why a different path is more aligned with who you are. Finding compromises that honor both your values and their expectations can help bridge the gap.

By applying these strategies and examples, you can effectively overcome obstacles that might hinder your journey to living authentically in alignment with your core values and self-identity. Remember that it's okay to face challenges; what matters is how you navigate them while staying true to yourself.

Celebrating Positive Changes

Living in alignment with your values can lead to positive changes in various aspects of your life. Celebrate these changes as they occur. Recognize the progress you've made, no matter how small, and use it as motivation to continue your journey towards an authentic life.

7

OVERCOMING OBSTACLES

Introduction

In this chapter, we're going to dive into some powerful strategies to help you tackle the things that have been bugging you, hold you back, or make you feel anxious. We'll break it down into three awesome parts, each inspired by our 3 friends: CBT, ACT, and DBT.

Section 1: Facing Your Fears (CBT)

Welcome to Section 1, where we're diving into the world of CBT (Cognitive Behavioral Therapy) to tackle those fears head-on. When it comes to facing fears, CBT is all about recognizing that the thoughts running through your mind can sometimes make you feel anxious or scared.

Imagine your thoughts as the director of a movie, and your feelings and actions are the actors on the screen. Sometimes, the director (your thoughts) might be telling the actors (your feelings and actions) to act scared or anxious. But guess what? You can change the script!

In this section, we'll be your scriptwriters, rewriting those scary scenes into empowering ones. We'll help you name your fears, create a ladder to climb one step at a time, and take baby steps to build your courage. And the best part? You'll learn how to flip the script on those negative thoughts and transform them into thoughts that help you conquer your fears.

Fear Busters: Learning How To Deal With Those Scary Feelings That Hold You Back.

We know that feeling scared or anxious is something everyone experiences from time to time. But what's even cooler is that we all have the power to take charge and confront those fears. In this section, we're going to become true Fear Busters!

Imagine your fear as a dragon guarding a treasure chest of opportunities and adventures. To claim your treasure, you'll need to learn how to face your fears head-on and show them who's boss. Don't worry; you've got this!

- **Fear Check-In:** Before we embark on our fear-busting journey, let's take a moment to check in with ourselves. What scares you the most right now? Is it speaking in front of a class, making new friends, or trying out for the school team? Maybe it's something else entirely. Whatever it is, it's perfectly okay to feel scared. We all do sometimes.

Imagine you have a secret journal where you can jot down your fears. Write it down, sketch it out, or even use emojis if that's more your style. This fear check-in is like putting on your armor before a big adventure. It helps us understand what's been holding you back and where we need to focus our fear-busting powers.

Now, to make this journey even more relatable, let's explore three scenarios that we'll use throughout this section. Meet Sarah, Alex, and Maya, our brave fear-busting trio:

- **Sarah's Stage Fright:** Sarah has always had a passion for singing, but the idea of performing in front of her classmates makes her heart race. She's terrified of messing up in front of everyone.

- **Alex's Social Butterfly Challenge:** Alex is outgoing and loves meeting new people, but every time he's about to approach someone new, he gets butterflies in his stomach. It's hard for him to start conversations.

- **Maya's Adventure Anxiety:** Maya dreams of going on thrilling adventures like zip-lining or rock climbing, but just thinking about it makes her palms sweaty. She's afraid of heights and taking risks.

Throughout this section, we'll follow Sarah, Alex, and Maya as they learn to conquer their fears, and you'll see how the techniques we explore can be applied to your own challenges.

Fear Journal: Just like our brave trio of Sarah, Alex, and Maya, it's time to grab your trusty Fear Journal. Think of it as your magical tool for understanding your fears better. Find a quiet spot, get your favorite journal or a piece of paper, and let's dive in.

- **Sarah's Fear Journal:** Sarah opens her journal and writes down, "I'm afraid of singing in front of my classmates because I might mess up and they'll laugh at me."

- **Alex's Fear Journal:** Alex jots down, "I'm scared to start conversations with new people because they might think I'm weird or boring."

- **Maya's Fear Journal:** Maya takes a deep breath and writes, "I'm anxious about heights and adventure activities because I'm scared of falling and getting hurt."

Now it's your turn. Don't hold back! Write down anything and everything that makes you feel uneasy. The Fear Journal is a safe space where you can be honest with yourself about what's been lurking in the shadows. Remember, naming your fears is the first step toward understanding and conquering them.

In the next steps, we'll use these named fears to create your very own Fear Ladder and start taking those fearless steps toward overcoming them.

Fear Ladder: Making a list from "meh" to "yikes" to tackle your fears step by step.

Sarah's Fear Ladder:

1. Sing a song in your room when no one's around (meh).

2. Sing a song in front of a trusted friend (a bit scarier).

3. Sing a song in front of a small group of friends (getting braver).

4. Sing a song in front of your family (a little scarier).

5. Sing a song in front of your whole class (yikes!).

Alex's Fear Ladder:

1. Smile at a stranger in the hallway (meh).

2. Say "hi" to a classmate you don't know well (a bit scarier).

3. Start a conversation with a friend of a friend (getting braver).

4. Join a club or group and introduce yourself (a little scarier).

5. Give a short speech or presentation in front of your class (yikes!).

Maya's Fear Ladder:

1. Stand on a low platform (meh).

2. Climb a short ladder or stairs (a bit scarier).

3. Walk across a sturdy bridge (getting braver).

4. Try indoor rock climbing (a little scarier).

5. Go ziplining or try an outdoor adventure activity (yikes!).

Now it's your turn! Create your very own Ladder of Courage, listing your fears from the least scary (meh) to the most intimidating (yikes). This ladder will serve as your guide, helping you take those brave steps forward. Remember, every step you climb brings you closer to conquering your fears and unlocking incredible opportunities. So, let's start climbing that ladder of courage together!

- **Baby Steps:** Taking small steps to face fears and build confidence.

Now that we've got your Fear Ladder in place, it's time to put on your explorer boots and take those first steps. We're not leaping into the deep end just yet; instead, we'll start with baby steps to build your confidence and prove to yourself that you're way stronger than your fears.

Imagine these baby steps as your trusty map for this journey. They're like the stepping stones across a river, helping you reach the other side. Each step is a victory that brings you closer to your goal.

- **Fear Tackling Plan:** Just like our fearless trio, let's pick one fear from your Fear Ladder that feels manageable right now. Remember, we're starting small and working our way up. What's the smallest step you can take to face that fear? Write it down in your Fear Tackling Plan, and let's make a strategy to conquer it.

Sarah's Fear Tackling Plan:

Fear: Singing a song in your room when no one's around (meh).

Step 1: Choose a song you love.

Step 2: Close your bedroom door.

Step 3: Sing along to the music with confidence.

Step 4: Celebrate your solo performance!

Alex's Fear Tackling Plan:

Fear: Smiling at a stranger in the hallway (meh).

Step 1: Make eye contact and smile at a friendly-looking person.

Step 2: Start with a simple "hello" or a nod.

Step 3: See how they respond and continue the conversation if it feels right.

Step 4: Feel the confidence growing with each interaction.

Maya's Fear Tackling Plan:

Fear: Standing on a low platform (meh).

Step 1: Find a small platform or step.

Step 2: Place one foot on it.

Step 3: Balance and take a deep breath.

Step 4: Step down with a proud smile—small victory achieved!

Now it's your turn! Choose one fear from your ladder that feels manageable right now (remember, we're starting at the "meh" level), and let's create your Fear Tackling Plan. Writing it down is like marking the path on your map, and together, we'll make sure you reach your destination—one confident step at a time. Ready to take your first baby step? Let's do this!

- **Flip the Script:** Changing your scary thoughts into positive ones.

Now that we've tackled naming your fears, creating your Fear Ladder, and taking those brave baby steps, it's time to deal with the thoughts that can sometimes make those steps feel challenging.

Imagine your thoughts as the storytellers of your adventure. They can make the journey seem scarier or more exciting. It's time to become the author of your own fearless story by flipping the script on those scary thoughts and turning them into positive, empowering beliefs.

- **Fear-Flipping Practice:** Just like our brave trio, when you catch yourself thinking those fearful thoughts, it's time to take a moment and challenge them. Are they really true, or are they just stories your mind is telling you? Can you find evidence to the contrary that shows you're stronger than you think?

Sarah's Fear-Flipping Practice:

Fear: "I might mess up singing in front of my classmates, and they'll laugh at me."

- **Challenge**: Have I ever sung perfectly every time? No. Everyone makes mistakes sometimes.

- **Flip the Script:** "I might make a mistake while singing, but that's okay. Everyone makes mistakes, and it doesn't define me."

Alex's Fear-Flipping Practice:

Fear: "People will think I'm weird or boring if I start conversations with them."

- **Challenge:** Have I ever met someone new who was boring or weird to me? Probably not.

- **Flip the Script:** "Starting conversations with new people can lead to awesome connections. They might find me interesting and cool!"

Maya's Fear-Flipping Practice:

Fear: "I'm scared of falling and getting hurt during adventure activities."

- **Challenge**: Have I seen people safely enjoy these activities? Yes, many times.

- **Flip the Script:** "Adventure activities are thrilling, and I can do them safely. I'll have an incredible time, and the fear won't hold me back."

Now, it's your turn! Whenever you catch yourself thinking those fearful thoughts, take a deep breath and challenge them. Are they really true? Can you find evidence to prove them wrong? Practice flipping your thoughts into positive ones, and remember, you're the author of your fearless story. Let's keep flipping those scripts and embracing the adventure ahead!

Facing Your Fears Worksheet

Fear Check-In:

1. Take a moment to reflect on what scares you the most right now. It can be anything, big or small.

Example: Fear of speaking in front of a group.

Name Your Fear:

2. Now, let's dig a little deeper. What's been giving you the jitters? Be specific about the fear you've identified.

Example: Fear of messing up my speech and embarrassing myself.

Fear Ladder:

3. Think about your fear on a scale from "meh" to "yikes." What are the different levels of this fear, from the least scary to the most intimidating?

Example:

- *"Meh" Level: Speaking confidently in front of a mirror.*

- *"A Bit Scarier" Level: Presenting in front of a small group of friends.*

- *"Getting Braver" Level: Speaking in a class with some familiar faces.*

- *"A Little Scarier" Level: Presenting in front of your whole class.*

- *"Yikes!" Level: Speaking at a school assembly.*

Baby Steps:

4. Choose one fear from your Fear Ladder that feels manageable right now, at the "meh" level. What's the smallest step you can take to face it.

Example: Speaking confidently in front of a mirror.

Flip the Script:

5. Identify the fearful thought associated with the chosen fear. What scary thought makes it scarier than it needs to be?

Example: "I'll look silly talking to myself in the mirror."

6. Challenge your fearful thought. Is it really true? Can you find evidence to the contrary?

Example: I've practiced speeches before, and it's a common technique. It's not silly at all.

7. Now, flip the script. Turn your fearful thought into a positive and empowering belief.

Example: "Practicing in front of the mirror is a smart way to improve my speaking skills, and it shows dedication."

Congratulations! You've completed the "Facing Your Fears" worksheet. Remember, this is a tool to help you understand and conquer your fears step by step. Keep using it to build your courage and move forward fearlessly!

Song Recommendation: "Eye of the Tiger" by Survivor

Section 2: Radical Acceptance (DBT)

Welcome to Section 2: Radical Acceptance! In this part of our journey, we're going to dive deep into the powerful concept of Radical Acceptance, a key component of Dialectical Behavior Therapy (DBT).

Why Radical Acceptance?

Life isn't always a smooth ride. There are times when things don't go as planned, and that's where Radical Acceptance comes in. It's about acknowledging the facts of a situation, even when they're tough to swallow. It doesn't mean you have to like or agree with everything that happens, but it's a way to find peace and move forward.

How Can Radical Acceptance Help?

- **Reduces Emotional Suffering:** When we resist reality, we often create additional emotional pain for ourselves. Radical Acceptance can help reduce this suffering by letting go of the struggle.

- **Enhances Resilience:** By accepting the challenges life throws at us, we become more resilient. We can adapt and bounce back more effectively.

- **Improves Relationships:** Accepting others as they are, flaws and all, can lead to healthier and more compassionate relationships.

- **Promotes Mindfulness:** Radical Acceptance is closely tied to mindfulness, which helps us stay present, grounded, and less reactive in challenging situations.

- **Supports Emotional Regulation:** It can be a powerful tool for managing intense emotions, allowing us to respond more skillfully rather than reactively.

Radical Chill: Discovering the Art of Just Rolling with It When Things Don't Go Your Way

In this section, we're going to delve into the art of "Radical Chill." It's all about staying cool, collected, and unruffled in the face of life's curveballs.

The Steps of Radical Chill

Step 1: Acknowledge the Situation

- When something unexpected or challenging happens, take a moment to acknowledge it. Avoid denying or avoiding the reality of the situation.

Step 2: Breathe and Ground Yourself

- Practice mindful breathing to stay grounded. Take deep breaths in and out, allowing yourself to let go of tension and anxiety.

Step 3: Reframe Your Perspective

- Shift your mindset from resisting the situation to accepting it as a part of life. Consider it as an opportunity for growth and learning.

Step 4: Choose Your Response

- Instead of reacting impulsively, choose a response that aligns with your values and goals. This step empowers you to make decisions consciously.

Step 5: Practice Self-Compassion

- Be kind to yourself. Understand that everyone faces challenges, and it's okay not to have all the answers. Treat yourself with the same compassion you would offer a friend in a similar situation.

Scenarios

Scenario 1: Family Gathering Frustration

Scenario: Your family is hosting a big gathering at your home, and things start going wrong. The food isn't ready on time, and your relatives are getting impatient.

- **Application of Radical Chill:** You acknowledge the situation, take deep breaths to stay calm, reframe your perspective by seeing it as an opportunity for family bonding, choose to communicate openly, and practice self-compassion if things don't go perfectly.

- **Consequence of Not Applying Radical Chill:** Without Radical Chill, you might react with frustration and anger, leading to strained family relationships and a stressful atmosphere.

Scenario 2: Friend's Change of Plans

Scenario: Your best friend cancels your weekend plans at the last minute because of a sudden commitment.

- **Application of Radical Chill:** You acknowledge the change in plans, take deep breaths to stay composed, reframe your perspective by understanding that unexpected events happen, choose to be understanding, and practice self-compassion by finding alternative activities.

- **Consequence of Not Applying Radical Chill:** Without Radical Chill, you might react with disappointment and resentment, causing tension in your friendship and ruining your weekend.

Scenario 3: Unexpected School Project Twist

Scenario: Your group project partner unexpectedly drops out of the project, leaving you with extra work to do.

- **Application of Radical Chill:** You acknowledge the change in circumstances, take deep breaths to stay focused, reframe your perspective by seeing it as an opportunity to showcase your skills, choose to communicate with your teacher, and practice self-compassion by recognizing your efforts.

- **Consequence of Not Applying Radical Chill:** Without Radical Chill, you might panic or get overwhelmed, leading to lower-quality work and increased stress.

In these scenarios, Radical Chill empowers you to stay composed, make thoughtful decisions, and maintain healthy relationships, even when life throws unexpected challenges your way. Embracing this skill helps you navigate life's twists and turns with grace and resilience.

Letting Go: Figuring Out How to Accept the Stuff You Can't Change

In this section, we're delving into the art of "Letting Go." Life often presents us with situations we can't change, no matter how hard we try. Letting Go is about releasing the grip on what's beyond your control and finding peace in the process.

The Steps of Letting Go

Step 1: Identify What You Can't Change

- Begin by recognizing the aspects of the situation that you have no control over. This clarity is the first step toward acceptance.

Step 2: Acknowledge Your Emotions

- Allow yourself to feel whatever emotions arise. Emotions are a natural response to life's challenges, and it's okay to acknowledge them.

Step 3: Practice Radical Acceptance

- Apply the concept of Radical Acceptance by fully embracing the reality of the situation without resistance or judgment.

Step 4: Refocus Your Energy

- Redirect your energy and efforts toward things you can control. This could involve finding solutions within your control or engaging in self-care to manage your emotions.

Step 5: Seek Support

- Don't hesitate to reach out to friends, family, or professionals for support and guidance in processing your emotions and finding healthy ways to cope.

Scenarios

Scenario 1: Family Financial Strain

Scenario: Your family is experiencing financial difficulties due to unforeseen circumstances, and it's affecting your lifestyle.

- **Application of Letting Go:** You identify that you can't change the financial situation, acknowledge your anxiety and frustration, practice Radical Acceptance by accepting the reality, refocus your energy on helping your family adjust to the changes, and seek support from a school counselor.

- **Consequence of Not Applying Letting Go:** Without Letting Go, you might feel overwhelmed, resentful, or anxious, leading to strained family relationships and increased stress.

Scenario 2: Friend's Personal Choices

Scenario: Your close friend is making choices that you disagree with and feel are harmful to them.

- **Application of Letting Go:** You identify that you can't control your friend's choices, acknowledge your concern and worry, practice Radical Acceptance by accepting your friend's autonomy, refocus your energy on maintaining a supportive and open friendship, and seek support from a trusted adult if necessary.

- **Consequence of Not Applying Letting Go:** Without Letting Go, you might become frustrated or push your friend away, potentially damaging your friendship and causing emotional distress.

Scenario 3: Unpredictable School Schedule

Scenario: Your school schedule changes unexpectedly, affecting your extracurricular activities and study routine.

- **Application of Letting Go:** You identify that you can't change the school schedule, acknowledge your disappointment and frustration, practice Radical Acceptance by accepting the change, refocus your energy on adapting your study habits, and seek support from a teacher for guidance.

- **Consequence of Not Applying Letting Go:** Without Letting Go, you might resist the schedule change, leading to increased stress and hindrance to your academic performance.

In these scenarios, Letting Go empowers you to accept the things beyond your control, manage your emotions effectively, and find constructive ways to adapt and cope. Embracing this skill helps you maintain your well-being and navigate life's uncertainties with grace and resilience.

It's Not Agreeing: Realizing That Accepting Doesn't Mean You're Okay With It

In this section, we're diving into the concept of "It's Not Agreeing." Sometimes, accepting a situation doesn't mean you're endorsing or approving of it. It's about understanding that acceptance and agreement are not the same. You can acknowledge reality without condoning it. This skill empowers you to navigate situations where you might need to accept something you don't necessarily like.

The Steps of It's Not Agreeing

Step 1: Recognize the Difference

- Understand that accepting a situation is not the same as agreeing with it. Acceptance means acknowledging the reality without judgment.

Step 2: Validate Your Feelings

- Validate your emotions and feelings about the situation. It's okay to have a range of emotions, even if you don't agree with what's happening.

Step 3: Set Boundaries

- Determine your boundaries and values regarding the situation. What are your limits, and what behaviors or actions are not in alignment with your values?

Step 4: Communicate Clearly

- If necessary, express your thoughts and feelings to others involved in the situation. Communicate your boundaries and your perspective without hostility or judgment.

Step 5: Focus on Self-Care

- Engage in self-care practices to manage your emotions and well-being. Take steps to maintain your mental and emotional health.

Scenarios

Scenario 1: Family Decision Disagreement

Scenario: Your family makes a decision about a vacation destination that you strongly disagree with.

- **Application of It's Not Agreeing:** You recognize that accepting their decision doesn't mean you have to agree with it. You validate your frustration and disappointment, communicate your concerns respectfully, set boundaries for your participation in the vacation, and practice self-care to manage your emotions.

- **Consequence of Not Applying It's Not Agreeing:** Without this skill, you might engage in arguments or resentment, causing family conflicts and added stress.

Scenario 2: Friend's Controversial Opinion

Scenario: Your friend expresses a controversial opinion that you find offensive and strongly disagree with.

- **Application of It's Not Agreeing:** You acknowledge that accepting your friend's right to their opinion doesn't mean you agree with it. You validate your discomfort and communicate your boundaries about discussing sensitive topics, all while maintaining respect for your friend's autonomy.

- **Consequence of Not Applying It's Not Agreeing:** Without this skill, you might engage in heated arguments or distance yourself from your friend, potentially harming the friendship and causing emotional turmoil.

Scenario 3: School Policy Change

Scenario: Your school introduces a new policy that you believe is unfair and disagree with.

- **Application of It's Not Agreeing:** You understand that accepting the policy doesn't mean you approve of it. You validate your frustration, express your concerns through appropriate channels, and focus on advocating for change while abiding by the policy to maintain your academic progress.

- **Consequence of Not Applying It's Not Agreeing:** Without this skill, you might resist the policy and face disciplinary actions or emotional distress, potentially hindering your academic performance.

In these scenarios, "It's Not Agreeing" empowers you to accept situations while maintaining your values, boundaries, and emotional well-being. It enables you to navigate disagreements and conflicts with respect and assertiveness, fostering healthier relationships and effective communication.

Section 3: Making Changes Stick (ACT)

This section is all about taking what you've learned and putting it into action to create lasting change. Acceptance and Commitment Therapy (ACT) is all about accepting your thoughts and feelings, even the challenging ones, and then committing to actions aligned with your values.

Rock Your Values: Clarify What Truly Matters to You

In previous chapters, we introduced the concept of values as an essential component of Acceptance and Commitment Therapy (ACT). Values are the core principles and beliefs that define what truly matters to you in life. They serve as your North Star, guiding your decision-making process and providing a sense of purpose and direction.

Values as a Foundation for Overcoming Obstacles

Values play a pivotal role in helping you overcome obstacles, and here's how:

1. Clarity in Decision-Making: When you have a clear understanding of your values, you can make decisions that align with what's truly important to you. This clarity empowers you to navigate challenges by choosing actions that honor your values.

2. Motivation and Resilience: Your values act as a wellspring of motivation. When you encounter obstacles, knowing that your actions are in alignment with your values can provide the fuel to persevere. It strengthens your resilience, helping you bounce back from setbacks.

3. Prioritizing Goals: Values serve as a filter for setting and prioritizing goals. When facing multiple challenges, you can assess which goals are most in line with your values and focus your efforts accordingly.

4. Maintaining Authenticity: Staying true to your values during challenging times allows you to maintain authenticity and integrity. This authenticity can enhance your relationships and provide a solid foundation for problem-solving.

Scenario: Academic Pressure

Scenario: *You're facing a challenging academic semester with multiple assignments, exams, and projects. The pressure to perform well is high, and you're feeling overwhelmed.*

Application of "Rock Your Values":

Step 1: Clarify Your Values

- You take some time to reflect on your values. You identify that "learning" and "personal growth" are two of your core values. You value education and continuous improvement.

Step 2: Align with Your Values

- When you feel overwhelmed, you remind yourself that the reason you're pursuing education is to learn and grow. This realignment with your values shifts your perspective.

Step 3: Prioritize Your Well-Being

- While striving for academic excellence is important, you also recognize the value of self-care and maintaining your mental and physical health. You set boundaries to ensure you have time for relaxation and self-care activities.

Step 4: Seek Support

- You reach out to classmates and professors for assistance when needed, aligning with your value of "collaboration" and "asking for help."

Step 5: Bounce Back with Resilience

- When you face setbacks, like a lower-than-expected grade on an assignment, you remind yourself that it's an opportunity for growth. You embrace the challenge, knowing that learning from mistakes is aligned with your values.

By clarifying and aligning with your values, you find the motivation to persevere through the academic pressure. You maintain your well-being, seek support when needed, and bounce back from setbacks with resilience. This values-based approach not only helps you overcome the obstacles but also allows you to do so with a sense of purpose and personal growth.

"Rock Your Values" becomes your compass during this challenging academic journey, guiding you to make decisions and take actions that are in harmony with what truly matters to you.

De-Crazy Your Brain: Gain the Tools to Manage Intrusive Thoughts

In Section 3 of this workbook, we revisit essential concepts related to managing intrusive and negative thoughts. While you've encountered these tools in earlier chapters, this section provides a dedicated space to focus on integrating and applying them for effectively managing intrusive thoughts that can hinder your progress and well-being.

Mastering the Art of Thought Management

Negative and intrusive thoughts are like unwelcome guests that can disrupt your life and well-being. These thoughts often manifest as self-doubt, self-criticism, or irrational fears, and they can have a significant impact on your emotional state and actions.

Applying Familiar Tools to Manage Intrusive Thoughts

In "De-Crazy Your Brain," you'll revisit and refine the tools you've encountered before, specifically tailored to managing intrusive thoughts:

1. Mindfulness and Awareness: Reconnect with the practice of observing your thoughts without judgment. Mindfulness creates a space between you and your thoughts, allowing for greater perspective.

2. Cognitive Defusion: Build on your knowledge of recognizing and challenging cognitive distortions by delving deeper into the technique of cognitive defusion. This skill helps you detach from irrational thoughts by understanding that they are mental events rather than concrete truths.

3. Self-Compassion: Re-emphasize the importance of treating yourself with kindness and understanding, countering harsh self-criticism and promoting self-acceptance.

4. Thought Defusion Exercises: Engage in practical exercises to revisit and strengthen your ability to challenge and defuse negative thoughts, reducing their impact on your well-being.

5. Values-Based Action: Reconnect with the concept of aligning your actions with your values, creating a positive feedback loop that counteracts negative thinking patterns.

Scenario: Overcoming Self-Doubt

Scenario: *You have a big presentation coming up at school or work, and you start experiencing self-doubt. Negative thoughts like, "I'm not good enough" or "I'll mess up" flood your mind, causing anxiety.*

Application of "De-Crazy Your Brain" Tools:

Step 1: Mindfulness and Awareness

- You revisit the practice of mindfulness by observing your thoughts without judgment, acknowledging them without letting them define you.

Step 2: Cognitive Defusion

- You remind yourself that these thoughts are just mental events, not concrete facts, reinforcing the technique of cognitive defusion.

Step 3: Self-Compassion

- You apply self-compassion by reassuring yourself with kindness, saying, "It's okay to feel this way; everyone gets nervous sometimes."

Step 4: Thought Defusion Exercises" that focuses on reframing negative thoughts:

- You engage in a thought defusion exercise to challenge and reframe the negative thoughts. You practice mentally stepping back from your negative thoughts and seeing them as passing clouds in the sky. This shift in perspective helps you detach from these thoughts and reduces their impact on your self-esteem and confidence.

Step 5: Values-Based Action

- You reconnect with your values, such as "professional growth" or "helping others through your presentation," motivating you to take action despite self-doubt.

By revisiting and refining these tools, you regain control over your thoughts and emotions, allowing you to approach your presentation with more confidence. This chapter empowers you to manage intrusive thoughts effectively, promoting mental well-being and personal growth.

Facing Your Fears Worksheet

(Check out the sample responses at the end of the worksheet)

I love this! maybe italicize to make more noticable?

1. Fear or Challenge Description

Describe the fear or challenge you've chosen to address. Be specific about what it is and how it affects you.

2. CBT Approach (Cognitive Behavioral Therapy)

Identify any negative or unhelpful thoughts related to this fear or challenge. How can you challenge and reframe these thoughts?

3. ACT Approach (Acceptance and Commitment Therapy)

What values or personal aspirations are important to you in this situation? How can you commit to actions that align with these values despite the fear?

4. DBT Approach (Dialectical Behavior Therapy)

Consider any intense emotions that may arise while facing this fear or challenge. How can you use mindfulness and emotional regulation techniques to manage these emotions?

5. Action Plan

Outline specific steps or actions you will take to confront this fear or address the challenge. Be realistic and break it down into manageable steps.

Step 1:

Step 2:

Step 3:

6. Timeline:

Set a timeline for when you plan to complete each step of your action plan.

Step 1 (Date):

Step 2 (Date):

Step 3 (Date):

7. Anticipated Challenges

Identify any challenges or obstacles you might encounter while facing this fear or challenge. How will you address or overcome them?

Challenge 1:

Challenge 2:

Challenge 3:

8. Support System:

List individuals or resources that can provide support, guidance, or encouragement as you work on this fear or challenge.

Support Person 1:

Support Person 2:

Other Resources:

9. Reflection and Learning:

After taking action, reflect on your experience. Did you successfully face your fear or address the challenge? What did you learn about yourself and the strategies you used?

Here's a sample response for a fear or challenge related to school:

1. Fear or Challenge Description

I'm dealing with the fear of speaking up in class discussions. It's a big deal because I have important thoughts to share, but I get super nervous when I think about speaking in front of everyone. It's affecting my grades and making me feel left out in class.

2. CBT Approach (Cognitive Behavioral Therapy)

My negative thought is that everyone will judge me or think I'm dumb if I say something wrong. To challenge this, I'll remind myself that everyone makes mistakes, and my classmates are probably more focused on their own thoughts than judging me.

3. ACT Approach (Acceptance and Commitment Therapy

My value in this situation is learning and participating in class. Despite the fear, I'll commit to raising my hand and sharing my ideas because it's important to me.

4. DBT Approach (Dialectical Behavior Therapy)

I often get anxious when I think about speaking up. To manage these emotions, I'll practice deep breathing before class discussions and use mindfulness techniques to stay present.

5. Action Plan

Step 1: Start by sharing one comment or question in a smaller class where I feel more comfortable.

Step 2: Gradually increase participation to at least one comment per class, even in bigger classes.

Step 3: Seek feedback from my teacher to improve my speaking skills.

6. Timeline

Step 1 (Date): Next week's smaller class.

Step 2 (Date): Within a month.

Step 3 (Date): By the end of the semester.

7. Anticipated Challenges

Challenge 1: Fear of stumbling over my words.

Challenge 2: Worrying about what others think.

Challenge 3: Nervousness before each discussion.

I'll address these challenges by practicing speaking and focusing on the importance of learning over others' opinions.

8. Support System

Support Person 1: My friend Sarah, who is also working on speaking up.

Support Person 2: The school counselor for tips on managing anxiety.

Other Resources: Online articles and videos about public speaking.

9. Reflection and Learning

After facing this fear and participating in class discussions, I learned that it's not as scary as I thought. People are generally supportive, and I've gained confidence in my speaking abilities. Plus, I've realized that my opinions are valuable in class.

Remember that facing your fears is a courageous step towards personal growth, and you have the knowledge and resilience to do it. Best of luck on your journey to overcome obstacles and achieve your goals!

8

MAKING CHANGES LAST

Introduction

This chapter is all about giving you the tools to make the positive changes you've made throughout this workbook stick around for the long haul. We're going to use a blend of strategies inspired by CBT, ACT, and DBT to help you do just that.

In this chapter, we'll break things down into sections, each tackling a different aspect of making changes last. Here's a sneak peek:

Section 1: Relapse Prevention (CBT): We'll start by diving into how to prevent any slips or setbacks. It's like having a safety net to keep you on track.

Section 2: Values-based Living (ACT): Next, we'll explore how to connect your personal values with your actions, helping you stay committed to your goals.

Section 3: Behavioral Activation (CBT) and Building Mastery (DBT): Then, we'll look at how staying active and continuously learning new skills can help you maintain your progress.

Section 4: Bringing it All Together: Finally, we'll show you how these strategies all work together seamlessly to support your journey of lasting change.

So, let's dive in and equip you with the skills to make your positive changes stick around. We're here to help you keep that momentum going strong!

Section 1: Relapse Prevention (CBT)

We'll explore how Cognitive Behavioral Therapy (CBT) techniques can help you maintain the progress you've made so far. Think of it as a toolkit to keep you on the path to positive change.

Understanding Relapse Prevention: It's Like Skateboarding

Let's dive into relapse prevention with a real-world scenario. Imagine you're a skateboarder, and you're working hard to master a challenging trick—let's say it's a kickflip. You've been practicing for weeks, and you're getting really good at it. You can land the trick more often than not, and you're feeling proud of your progress.

One day, while practicing at your favorite skatepark, you hit a snag. You attempt the kickflip, but this time, you lose your balance, and you take a tumble. It's frustrating, and you feel a bit discouraged. That's your setback—a small one, but it feels like a setback nonetheless.

Now, let's relate this to relapse prevention. In this scenario, the kickflip is like the positive changes you've been making in your life, whether it's improving your grades, managing your emotions better, or building better relationships with your friends and family. You've been doing well, but setbacks, like falling off your skateboard, can happen to anyone.

Relapse prevention is like wearing protective gear when you skate. It includes your helmet, knee and elbow pads, and wrist guards. Just as this gear is designed to minimize the impact of falls and keep you safe, relapse prevention strategies are designed to minimize the impact of setbacks and help you stay on track with your positive changes.

When you understand relapse prevention, it's like knowing how to react when you lose your balance on your skateboard. You might get up, dust yourself off, and try the trick again. You don't give up just because you had a small setback. In the same way, relapse prevention helps you bounce back from setbacks and keep moving forward on your journey of personal growth.

So, even if you experience a hiccup along the way, relapse prevention strategies are your safety net, your way of saying, "I've got this!" You'll learn how to anticipate and manage those moments when things don't go as planned, and you'll keep riding towards your goals.

Identifying Common Triggers: Recognizing the Red Flags

Let's dive into the core of relapse prevention—identifying common triggers. Triggers as warning signs that signal potential challenges ahead. They come in various forms, and here are five scenarios that can help you recognize common triggers:

- **The Stressful Situation:** Picture this—you've got a big exam coming up, and the pressure is building. Stress can trigger a setback by making you feel overwhelmed, anxious, or even a bit scattered.

- **The Emotional Rollercoaster:** Imagine you've had a tough day, and you're feeling down. Negative emotions, like anger, sadness, or frustration, can sneak in and tempt you to revert to old habits as a way to cope.

- **The Peer Pressure Moment:** You're hanging out with a group of friends who don't really support your positive changes. Peer pressure is the trigger here. It can make you feel torn between fitting in and staying true to your goals.

- **The Boredom Blues:** It's a lazy weekend, and you've got nothing to do. Boredom can be a sneaky trigger. When you're not occupied, you might be tempted to revert to old behaviors just to pass the time.

- **The Family Tensions:** You're at home, and there's tension in the air. Family stress is the trigger in this scenario. It can create a challenging environment that tests your commitment to your positive changes.

- **Recognizing Triggers is Key:** The first step in relapse prevention is spotting these triggers when they appear. It's like having a radar that goes off, warning you, "Hey, watch out, potential setback ahead!"

- **Your Personal Triggers:** Triggers can vary from person to person. What stresses you out might not bother someone else, and that's perfectly okay. That's why it's crucial to get to know your own triggers—the things that make you go, "Uh-oh, I might slip up."

In the next sections, we'll explore what to do when these triggers pop up and how to build your personalized toolkit to stay ahead of them. So, let's keep going!

Early Warning Signs: Staying Ahead of the Game

In this section, we're delving into early warning signs—your allies in staying on track and preventing setbacks. It's like having a built-in alarm system that lets you know when you might be veering off course.

- **The Stress-o-Meter:** Picture a time when stress is piling up, and it's affecting your daily life. Early warning signs might include trouble sleeping, increased tension in your body, or a racing mind.

- **The Emotional Barometer:** Imagine feeling a surge of negative emotions like frustration or anger. Early warning signs could be clenched fists, a racing heart, or a knot in your stomach. These physical reactions are signals that you might need to take action.

- **The Peer Pressure Indicator:** You're in a situation where peer pressure is pushing you in a direction that doesn't align with your goals. Early warning signs could be feeling a pit in your stomach, doubting yourself, or experiencing a sense of inner conflict.

- **The Boredom Beacon:** During a dull moment, boredom starts to creep in. Early warning signs might include restlessness, a sense of aimlessness, or that feeling of "I should be doing something."

- **The Family Tensions Signal:** At home, you sense tension building up. Early warning signs could be changes in your communication style, increased irritability, or a feeling of walking on eggshells.

- **Listening to Your Body and Mind:** Pay close attention to physical and emotional signals—your body and mind are excellent at sending you messages. When you notice these signs, it's your cue to step back, take a breath, and decide on a course of action.

Coping Strategies: Building Your Toolkit

Now, we're delving into coping strategies—your trusty toolkit for managing triggers and preventing setbacks. Coping strategies are like having a toolbox filled with helpful gadgets. Each tool is designed to address specific challenges. Here are five scenarios that can help you understand how these strategies can work:

- **The Stress-Buster Tool:** When stress is looming large, coping strategies might include relaxation techniques like deep breathing, mindfulness, or visualization. These tools can help calm your mind and reduce stress.

- **The Emotion Management Kit:** When faced with intense negative emotions, coping strategies could involve techniques like journaling, talking to a trusted friend, or practicing self-compassion. These tools help you process and manage your feelings constructively.

- **The Peer Pressure Defense:** In situations involving peer pressure, coping strategies may include assertiveness training to help you express your thoughts and feelings confidently and respectfully. These tools empower you to stand your ground while maintaining healthy relationships.

- **The Boredom Breaker Arsenal:** When boredom strikes, coping strategies could involve finding engaging activities, setting goals, or practicing mindfulness to stay present and content. These tools help you ward off boredom without resorting to old habits.

- **The Family Harmony Toolkit:** In times of family tensions, coping strategies might include active listening, effective communication skills, or conflict resolution techniques. These tools promote understanding and maintain a peaceful environment.

Personalized Relapse Prevention Plan

You'll create a personalized relapse prevention plan tailored to your unique needs. This plan will include specific actions and strategies you can put into action if you ever feel like you're slipping.

Step 1: Identify Your Triggers

Think about situations or emotions that have led to setbacks in the past. Which triggers are most likely to challenge your progress?

Sample Response:

Triggers: *Stress, negative emotions, and peer pressure*

```



```

Step 2: Recognize Early Warning Signs

What physical or emotional signals do you notice when you're approaching a potential setback? How does your body or mind alert you?

Sample Response:

Early Warning Signs: *Racing thoughts, increased heart rate, and irritability*

```



```

Step 3: Select Coping Strategies

From the coping strategies we discussed, which ones do you think would work best for you in handling your specific triggers and early warning signs?

Sample Response: take out?

Coping Strategies: *Deep breathing exercises, journaling, and assertiveness training*

Step 4: Action Steps for Prevention

What specific actions can you take when you notice your triggers or early warning signs? How can you address them before they escalate?

Sample Response:

Action Steps:

- *When stressed, practice deep breathing for 5 minutes.*

- *Journal to process and manage negative emotions.*

- *Assertively communicate my boundaries and goals when facing peer pressure.*

Step 5: Reach Out for Support

Who can you reach out to for support when you face challenges? How can you communicate your needs to them effectively?

Sample Response:

Support Network: Close friend, family member, and therapist

Communication: Clearly express my feelings and request their understanding and encouragement.

Step 6: Review and Adjust

How often will you review and adjust your relapse prevention plan? What criteria will you use to determine if changes are necessary?

Sample Response:

Review Frequency: Monthly

Criteria for Adjustment: If I experience setbacks or if I notice my coping strategies aren't as effective.

Step 7: Commitment and Motivation

What keeps you motivated to work on your goals, even in the face of challenges? How will you stay committed to your relapse prevention plan?

Sample Response:

Motivation: *The desire for personal growth and a healthier, happier life.*

Commitment: *Remind myself of my goals daily and visualize the positive outcomes.*

Section 2: Values for Lasting Change

Welcome to Section 2, where we'll explore a crucial facet of your journey – making lasting changes through the lens of Acceptance and Commitment Therapy (ACT).

As we dive into this section, it's important to note that what we're about to explore is not entirely new. You've already learned about Acceptance and Commitment Therapy (ACT) in earlier chapters, which is a powerful approach to making lasting changes in your life.

Committed Action: Aligning Your Choices with Your Values

Committed action, a fundamental concept in ACT, involves taking consistent and purposeful steps in alignment with your core values. It's like having your values as your co-pilots on the journey of change. Here's how you can think of it:

1. **Identify Your Values-Aligned Goals (A Review):** You've already identified your core values, which are the compass guiding your choices. Take a moment to review your goals and ask yourself, "Do these goals reflect my core values?" If they don't, it's time to adjust them.

2. **Create an Action Plan (A Review):** Just as you've learned in ACT, break down your goals into actionable steps. These steps should be in harmony with your values.

3. **Daily Commitment (A Review):** Similar to ACT, make a daily commitment to living your values through your actions. Pledge to embody your values in your daily choices.

4. **Overcoming Challenges (A Review):** ACT teaches us that challenges are a part of the journey. When they arise, remember your core values as your guiding lights. They provide strength and direction when you face obstacles.

5. **Reflect and Adjust (A Review):** Periodically review your progress. Are your actions in line with your values? Are you making a meaningful impact? If adjustments are needed, refine your action plan to stay on course.

6. **Celebrate Success (A Review):** Just as in ACT, celebrating your achievements is a way of acknowledging the impact of your values-driven actions and reinforcing your commitment.

So, why look at it again? Because, as with any valuable tool, revisiting and deepening your understanding can provide fresh insights and reinforce its effectiveness. As you put your values into action, you'll find that your journey towards lasting change becomes not just meaningful but also highly rewarding.

Values and Mindfulness: A Recipe for Making Change Stick

Now, here's why bringing mindfulness and values together is super cool:

- **Super Awareness:** When you practice mindfulness, you become super aware of your thoughts, feelings, and actions in the moment. It's like turning on the lights in a dark room. You can see everything more clearly, including whether you're living up to your values or not.

- **Values in Action:** Your values are like your action plan. They tell you how to act and make choices that match what's really important to you. So, when you use mindfulness to pay attention to your values, you start doing things that line up with your personal code.

Now, for Real-Life Examples

Scenario 1: The Empathy Enthusiasts

Imagine your value is "empathy," and you want to be someone who deeply understands and supports others. Sometimes, in the hustle and bustle of life, you might not pay enough attention to people's feelings. That's where mindfulness comes to the rescue. It helps you tune in and notice those moments when you could be more empathetic, like when your friend seems upset. So, you remember your value ("empathy") and decide to actively listen and offer a comforting shoulder. Over time, you become one of the "Empathy Enthusiasts" because your friends know they can count on your genuine understanding and support.

Scenario 2: The Integrity Innovators

Let's say your value is "integrity," and you want to be known for your honesty and doing what's right, even when it's tough. Life often throws tricky situations your way, where bending the truth might seem tempting. This is when mindfulness steps in. It helps you recognize those moments when you could compromise your integrity, like when you're tempted to copy someone's homework. So, you remember your value ("integrity") and choose the honest path, even if it means putting in extra effort. As time goes on, you become one of the "Integrity Innovators" because you're unwavering in your commitment to doing what's right.

In this section, you've discovered how values are your key to making lasting changes. We've highlighted their significance in your journey.

Section 3: Building Lasting Change through Action

In this section, we'll explore two potent strategies, Behavioral Activation (CBT) and Building Mastery (DBT), that lay the groundwork for creating lasting change. By harnessing the principles of these therapeutic approaches, you'll learn how to turn intentions into actions and sustain positive changes effectively.

Now, let's dive into these strategies, starting with "Identifying Meaningful Activities."

Identifying Meaningful Activities

One key to making lasting change is identifying activities that resonate with you, bringing a sense of fulfillment and purpose. These activities are the building blocks of lasting change.

How It Relates to DBT and CBT

- **Behavioral Activation (CBT)**: In CBT, we've got this cool thing called Behavioral Activation. It's all about finding and doing stuff that makes you feel awesome. So, when you pick meaningful activities that boost your mood and make you happier, you're basically rocking Behavioral Activation, CBT style!

- **Building Mastery (DBT):** In DBT, they talk about Building Mastery, which is like leveling up your skills and confidence. When you choose activities that challenge you and help you grow, you're totally in sync with Building Mastery, DBT's superhero move for becoming more awesome.

Step by Step:

1. Why It's So Cool: Start by understanding why picking activities that matter is a big deal. It's like choosing your own adventure in life, making sure it's filled with happiness and things that light your fire.

- *Example: Imagine you're crazy about gaming. Knowing why it's cool would mean realizing that gaming isn't just fun; it's your ticket to having a blast and growing as a person.*

2. Unleash Your Inner Excitement: Take a moment to unleash your inner excitement and think about what really gets you pumped. What activities make you feel like you're on cloud nine?

- *Example: If you're all about music, this step means getting stoked about those jam sessions, concerts, or even just playing your favorite tunes on the guitar.*

3. Goals That Rock: Now, think about what you want to achieve with these awesome activities. Goals give your actions a purpose and a target to aim for.

- *Example: Let's say you're into skateboarding. Your goal might be to master a new trick or even become a skateboarding legend in your neighborhood.*

4. Start Small, Go Big: Don't rush it! Begin by adding these cool activities into your daily life in baby steps. When you feel confident, you can crank up the volume.

- *Example: If you're into art, you might begin with doodling in a notebook. Once you're feeling like the Picasso of your generation, you can tackle larger canvases.*

5. Embrace the Awesome: Remember, it's all about embracing the awesomeness of these activities. When you're doing them, it's not just a chore; it's a chance to be your most awesome self.

- *Example: Let's say you're crazy about coding. Embracing the awesome means realizing that coding isn't just lines of text; it's your superpower to create amazing things.*

Overcoming Barriers to Engagement

In this part of our journey, we'll tackle the challenges that may obstruct your path to lasting change. These barriers can manifest as procrastination, low motivation, or self-doubt, hindering your progress. By implementing strategies rooted in Behavioral Activation (CBT) and Building Mastery (DBT) principles, you'll learn to overcome these obstacles effectively.

Step by Step:

1. Spot Those Hurdles: First things first, let's spot those sneaky barriers that are trying to rain on your parade. These can be things like putting things off, doubting yourself, or feeling like you're stuck in a motivation desert.

- *Example: Imagine you've got a big project due, and procrastination is your sworn enemy. Spotting the hurdle means recognizing that procrastination is the villain blocking your path.*

2. Realize the Impact: It's time to get real about how these hurdles mess with your groove. They can be like roadblocks on your journey to awesome. Acknowledge how they're stopping you from becoming your best self.

- *Example: When you see how procrastination keeps you from acing your projects and feeling proud of your work, you're understanding the impact.*

3. Super Strategies: Now, let's bust out some superhero moves to conquer these hurdles. Think like a CBT superhero and set clear goals, break tasks into smaller chunks, and make a game plan to defeat procrastination.

- *Example: Your superhero strategy is to set daily goals for your project, break it down into research, writing, and editing tasks, and make a schedule to stay on track.*

4. Mastering Mind Skills: Time to channel your inner Jedi with DBT's ninja skills. Build up your mental armor with positive self-talk, mindfulness tricks, and calling in reinforcements like mentors or friends when self-doubt strikes.

- *Example: When self-doubt creeps in, you use the Jedi mind trick of telling yourself, "I've got this," and practicing deep breathing exercises to stay focused.*

5. Get a Wingman (or Woman): Every hero needs a sidekick! Find a buddy or mentor who's got your back and will help you stay on the path to awesomeness. They'll cheer you on and make sure you don't slip.

- *Example: Your trusty sidekick is your best friend, who's always there to remind you of your goals and nudge you when procrastination tries to sneak in.*

Boosting Your Skills and Confidence

Getting better at something isn't just about gaining superpowers overnight. It's a journey, and it's all about leveling up your skills and confidence. Here's why it's super cool:

1. Unleash Your Potential: When you work on building mastery, you're basically unleashing your inner super-hero. You discover talents and skills you didn't even know you had, and that's seriously awesome.

2. Confidence Booster: Building mastery is like pumping up your confidence muscles. As you become better at things, you start believing in yourself more, and that can help you tackle any challenge that comes your way.

Steps for Building Confidence and Competence:

1. Setting Achievable Goals: Start by setting clear and achievable goals that challenge you but are realistic.

2. Breaking Goals into Steps: Divide larger goals into smaller, manageable steps to make progress more manageable.

3. Skill Development: Identify the skills needed to achieve your goals and invest time in developing them.

4. Regular Practice: Dedicate consistent time to practice and refine your skills.

5. Celebrate Accomplishments: Recognize and celebrate your achievements, no matter how small, to boost your self-confidence.

Now let's run through some scenarios.

Scenario 1: Becoming the Soccer Star

Imagine you're all about soccer, and you're determined to become the soccer superstar of your school.

Here's how you can apply the steps:

1. **Setting Achievable Goals:** Start by setting a clear goal, like scoring a certain number of goals in your next few games. It's a challenge, but it's doable.

2. **Breaking Goals into Steps:** Break down your big goal into smaller steps, like practicing your dribbling skills, improving your accuracy in shooting, and working on your ball control.

3. **Skill Development:** Focus on developing specific skills that matter in soccer, such as agility, speed, and precision in your kicks.

4. **Regular Practice:** Dedicate time each day to practice. Whether it's dribbling drills in your backyard or shooting goals at the local park, consistent practice is key.

5. **Celebrate Accomplishments:** Celebrate each milestone. When you score a fantastic goal in a game, do your victory dance, and share your success with your soccer buddies.

Scenario 2: Mastering the Art of Friendship

Let's say you're all about building strong friendships.

Here's how you can apply the steps:

1. **Setting Achievable Goals:** Start by setting a goal to make one new friend within the next month. It's challenging, but it's achievable!

2. **Breaking Goals into Steps:** Break down your friendship goal into smaller steps, like striking up conversations with classmates, inviting someone to join your lunch table, or attending social events.

3. **Skill Development:** Focus on developing communication skills, active listening, and empathy to connect with others effectively.

4. **Regular Practice:** Dedicate time to socialize regularly. Attend school events, join clubs, and say "hi" to new people. Practice makes perfect!

5. **Celebrate Accomplishments:** Celebrate each new friendship you make. Share a memorable moment with your new friend, like a fun outing or playing video games together.

Scenario 3: Acing the Math Challenges

Now, let's say you're all about conquering those tough math challenges at school.

Here's how you can apply the steps:

1. **Setting Achievable Goals:** Start by setting a goal to improve your math test scores by a specific percentage in the next semester. It's a challenge, but it's definitely achievable!

2. **Breaking Goals into Steps:** Break down your math goal into smaller steps, like practicing math problems daily, seeking help from your math teacher or a tutor, and staying organized with your math notes.

3. **Skill Development:** Focus on developing problem-solving skills, understanding mathematical concepts, and practicing critical thinking.

4. **Regular Practice:** Dedicate time each day to tackle math problems. The more you practice, the more confident you'll become.

5. **Celebrate Accomplishments:** Celebrate when you ace a challenging math test or solve a particularly tricky problem. Treat yourself to a favorite snack or share your success with your math-loving friends.

Combating Boredom and Apathy

This section addresses a critical aspect of creating lasting change – combating boredom and apathy. Boredom and apathy can be formidable foes on your path to lasting change. When you're bored, you're more likely to resort to unproductive or unhealthy habits to fill the void. These habits can be counterproductive and even detrimental to your progress. By combating boredom and apathy, you'll ensure that you stay engaged, motivated, and on track with your meaningful activities, reducing the risk of setbacks.

Common Habits Reflecting Boredom:

- Mindlessly scrolling through social media for hours.

- Excessive binge-watching of TV shows or movies.

- Procrastination and avoiding responsibilities.

- Overindulgence in unhealthy snacks or comfort eating.

- Spending excessive time in bed or aimlessly wandering the internet.

Step by Step:

1. Recognize the Signs: Begin by recognizing the signs of boredom and apathy in your life. This may include feelings of restlessness, disinterest in activities, or a lack of motivation.

- *Example: You notice that you're spending most of your free time mindlessly scrolling through social media, and your interest in your hobbies has dwindled.*

2. Identify Triggers: Explore what triggers your feelings of boredom and apathy. Is it a lack of challenging activities, a monotonous routine, or unmet needs?

- *Example: You realize that your boredom often strikes when you have free time with no plans or when you're not engaged in activities that interest you.*

3. Explore New Interests: Actively seek out new interests and hobbies that excite you. These can be related to your existing passions or entirely new endeavors.

- *Example: You decide to explore photography as a new hobby, signing up for a beginner's photography class.*

4. Set Structured Goals: Establish structured goals related to your new interests. Setting clear objectives and milestones provides a sense of purpose and direction.

- *Example: Your goal is to capture a series of photos showcasing the beauty of your local neighborhood within the next three months.*

5. Challenge Yourself: Introduce challenges and variety into your activities. This prevents monotony and keeps you engaged.

- *Example: In your photography journey, you challenge yourself to capture unique shots from different angles and lighting conditions.*

6. Social Engagement: Involve friends or like-minded individuals in your activities. Social engagement adds an element of accountability and can make activities more enjoyable.

- *Example: You invite a friend who shares your interest in photography to join you on photo walks and share tips and experiences.*

7. Practice Mindfulness: Incorporate mindfulness techniques to stay present and appreciate the richness of your experiences.

- *Example: During your photo walks, you practice mindfulness by focusing on the details of your surroundings, enhancing your appreciation for photography.*

By following these steps, you'll actively combat boredom and apathy, ensuring that your journey towards lasting change remains vibrant and engaging.

Combatting Boredom and Apathy Worksheet

Boredom and apathy can be obstacles on your journey to lasting change. This worksheet will help you identify signs of boredom, explore strategies to combat it, and stay engaged in meaningful activities. Remember, overcoming boredom is essential for maintaining progress and preventing setbacks.

Part 1: Recognize the Signs

1. Take a moment to reflect on your recent experiences. Have you felt bored or apathetic in any aspect of your life? Describe these situations.

Example: I've felt bored during my free time, especially on weekends when I have no plans or activities.

2. List the emotions or feelings associated with your boredom or apathy. (e.g., restlessness, disinterest, lack of motivation)

Example: Emotions associated with my boredom include restlessness and a lack of motivation to do anything productive.

Part 2: Identify Triggers

3. What do you believe triggers your feelings of boredom and apathy? Is it a specific situation, routine, or unmet needs?

Example: I think my boredom is triggered when I have unstructured free time with no plans, and I'm not engaged in activities I enjoy.

Part 3: Explore New Interests

4. Name one or more new interests or hobbies you'd like to explore to combat boredom.

Example: I'd like to explore painting as a new hobby.

5. What appeals to you about these new interests or hobbies?

Example: Painting appeals to me because it allows me to express my creativity and relax.

Part 4: Set Structured Goals

6. Write down a clear goal related to your new interest. What would you like to achieve within a specific timeframe?

Example: My goal is to complete my first acrylic painting within the next two months.

7. Break down your goal into smaller, manageable steps. What can you do to work toward this goal incrementally?

*Example: **Step 1:** Gather painting supplies. **Step 2:** Find beginner painting tutorials online. **Step 3:** Practice basic techniques.*

Part 5: Challenge Yourself

8. How can you introduce challenges or variety into your chosen activity to prevent boredom?

Example: To challenge myself in painting, I'll experiment with different techniques and styles, like abstract and landscape.

Part 6: Social Engagement

9. Are there friends or individuals who share your interest or hobby? How can you involve them to make your activity more enjoyable?

Example: My friend Sarah enjoys painting too. I'll invite her over for a painting session to exchange ideas and have fun together.

Part 7: Practice Mindfulness

10. How can you incorporate mindfulness techniques into your chosen activity to stay present and fully engage with it?

Example: During my painting sessions, I'll practice mindfulness by focusing on the colors, brush strokes, and the process itself, rather than rushing to finish.

Song Recommendation: "Can't Stop the Feeling" by Justin Timberlake

Alright, listen up! Mixing CBT, ACT, and DBT is like crafting the ultimate power-up in your favorite game. Think of it this way: you're taking on those pesky self-doubt monsters, discovering what lights a fire in your soul, and mastering your emotions like a boss.

But here's the deal: it's not a one-and-done deal. Nah, you gotta keep at it, just like in a game where you grind to level up. Why? 'Cause when you stick with it, you're building skills that stick around for the long haul.

So, why should you care? Imagine facing any challenge that comes your way with confidence and control. Pretty sweet, right? That's the magic of committing to these techniques for the long run. So, keep pushing, stay committed, and watch as you power up your life like never before!

9

MOVING FORWARD

Introduction

You're almost at the end of this lit workbook, where we're wrapping up your journey of self-discovery and growth. Chapter 9 is all about diving deep into taking action, building your own toolkit, and planning for what's next. We're talking about setting goals, finding ways to chillax, and boosting your vibes.

is this blank intentional? (kinda like it!

Section 1: Setting SMART Goals (ACT)

Alright, you've discovered a lot about yourself in this workbook, and it's time to use that wisdom to set some epic goals that truly matter to you. We've dived into various goal-setting approaches in earlier chapters, but one that's tried and true is making SMART goals. So, let's get into it!

1. Specific: Be clear about what you want to achieve.

- Ask yourself: What exactly do I want to accomplish? The more specific, the better.

2. Measurable: Figure out how you'll know when you've reached your goal.

- Think about: How can I measure my progress? What will success look like?

3. Achievable: Make sure it's something you can realistically do.

- Consider: Is this goal within my reach? Can I take steps to make it happen?

4. Relevant: Does it fit with your values and what matters most to you?

- Reflect on: Does this goal align with my personal values and what I care about?

5. Time-bound: Set a deadline to keep yourself on track.

- Define: When do you want to achieve this goal? Having a timeline is crucial.

Now, let's apply these SMART criteria with three examples:

1. Friends

- **Specific:** Host a small get-together with a few friends at my house.

- **Measurable:** Count how many friends attend.

- **Achievable:** Plan it and invite friends.

- **Relevant:** Strengthening friendships is important to me.

- **Time-bound:** Within the next month.

2. Family

- **Specific:** Spend at least 30 minutes each day playing a game or talking with my sibling.

- **Measurable:** Track daily interactions.

- **Achievable:** Dedicate time to it.

- **Relevant:** Improving my relationship with my sibling is a family value.

- **Time-bound:** Two weeks.

3. School

- **Specific:** Raise my math grade from a C to a B.

- **Measurable:** Track my grades.

- **Achievable:** Study and work on math regularly.

- **Relevant:** School success matters to me.

- **Time-bound:** By the end of the current grading period.

By following these steps and making your goals SMART, you'll have a clear roadmap for achieving what matters most to you in different areas of your life. It helps you stay focused, measure progress, and celebrate your successes along the way!

Section 2: Progressive Relaxation (DBT)

Life can be pretty stressful sometimes, right? Well, in this section, we're going to explore a fantastic relaxation technique that's not only great for chilling out and reducing anxiety but also has a special connection to Dialectical Behavior Therapy (DBT). It's called Progressive Relaxation, and it's super easy to do:

Step 1: Find a Comfortable Place

- Start by finding a quiet and comfortable place to sit or lie down. You want to be able to relax without any distractions.

Step 2: Begin with Your Toes

- Close your eyes (if you feel comfortable doing so).

- Focus your attention on your toes. Imagine them becoming warm and heavy.

- Squeeze your toes tightly for about 5 seconds. Really tense them up.

Step 3: Release the Tension

- Now, slowly and gently release the tension in your toes. Feel them relaxing completely.

Step 4: Move Up Your Body

- Shift your focus to your calves (the muscles in your lower legs).

- Squeeze your calf muscles for 5 seconds, then let go, allowing them to relax.

Step 5: Continue Upward

- Gradually work your way up your body, repeating this process with different muscle groups.

- Tense each muscle group for about 5 seconds and then release it.

- Move from your calves to your thighs, then to your stomach, chest, arms, and finally to your face and head.

Option: Listen to Calming Music

- If you prefer, you can listen to calming music or nature sounds while doing Progressive Relaxation. It can enhance the relaxation experience.

When Can This Help?

Progressive Relaxation can be incredibly useful in various situations:

1. Before a big test or presentation: To calm pre-test jitters and improve focus.

2. When feeling anxious or stressed: To ease tension and promote a sense of calm.

3. Before bedtime: To help you relax and fall asleep more easily.

4. After a long day: To unwind and release built-up tension.

5. During moments of high emotion: To regain control and composure.

Remember, this technique is not just about relaxation but also about strengthening your emotional resilience, making it a valuable tool in your DBT toolkit. The more you practice it, the better you'll become at using it to create moments of calm and emotional balance in your life.

Section 3: Positive Psychology (CBT/ACT)

Happiness is a big deal, right? In this part, we'll explore ways to boost your happiness and create positive experiences in your life. It's all about looking at the bright side of things.

1. Gratitude Journal

Keeping a Gratitude Journal is a simple yet powerful way to shift your focus to the positive aspects of your life. Here's how to do it:

- Every day, write down three things you're grateful for. These can be big or small, from a sunny day to a kind friend, as long as they bring you joy.

- *Example: "Today, I'm grateful for the laughter I shared with my friends during lunch, the beautiful sunset I saw on my evening walk, and the support I received from my family when I needed it."*

2. Acts of Kindness

Doing something nice for others not only brightens their day but also gives you a mood boost. Acts of kindness can be simple and make a big difference.

- Compliment a classmate on their outfit or a job well done.

- Help a family member with chores without being asked.

- Hold the door open for someone or let someone go ahead of you in line.

- *Example: You notice your classmate has been feeling down lately, so you compliment their presentation in front of the class. Your kind words make them smile and feel appreciated.*

3. Mindfulness for Happiness

- Mindfulness exercises from earlier chapters can significantly increase your overall sense of happiness. Here's how to use mindfulness to boost your mood:

- Practice mindfulness regularly by taking a few moments to breathe deeply and focus on your breath. This helps you stay present and appreciate the small, beautiful moments in life.

- *Example: You're walking in the park, and you pause to take a few deep breaths while admiring the colors of the leaves, the sounds of birds chirping, and the feeling of the breeze on your skin. This mindful moment fills you with a sense of calm and happiness.*

By incorporating these techniques into your life, you'll be on your way to becoming a happier, more positive you! Remember, happiness often comes from the simple joys and positive actions in our daily lives, and these practices can help you cultivate a more positive outlook.

Moving Forward Worksheet: Setting SMART Goals (ACT)

(Check out the sample responses are at the end of the worksheet)

1. Specific Goals

Identify a specific goal related to your life, whether it's about friends, family, school, or something else. Be as clear as possible.

Goal:

2. Measurable Progress

How will you measure your progress toward this goal? What will success look like?

Measurement:

3. Achievability

Consider the steps you need to take to achieve your goal. Is it realistic? If not, how can you make it achievable?

Achievability:

4. Relevance to Your Values

Does this goal align with your values and what matters most to you? Why is it important?

Relevance:

5. Time-Bound Deadline

Set a deadline for achieving this goal to keep yourself on track.

Deadline:

Here are sample responses for each section:

1. Specific Goals

- *Goal: Improve my grade in math from a C to a B by the end of the semester.*

2. Measurable Progress

- *Measurement: I will track my progress by keeping a record of my math test scores and homework grades. Success will be achieving an average of 85% or higher in math assignments.*

3. Achievability

- *Achievability: To make this goal achievable, I will dedicate at least 1 hour every day to studying math, seek help from my teacher or tutor when I encounter difficulties, and practice solving math problems regularly.*

4. Relevance to Your Values

- *Relevance: This goal aligns with my values because I value academic success and personal growth. Improving my math grade will not only boost my confidence but also open up opportunities for future academic and career pursuits that require strong math skills.*

5. Time-Bound Deadline

- *Deadline: I will achieve this goal by the end of the current semester, which is in three months' time. My deadline is May 30th.*

Creating Your Personal Toolbox

Discovering Your Strengths

In this section, take some time to reflect on your journey through this workbook. Think about the skills and strategies that have helped you the most. These could be specific exercises, coping techniques, or even insights you've gained about yourself.

Write down your strengths and positive qualities that have become evident during this process. These can include qualities like resilience, determination, empathy, or creativity.

Recognize how these strengths have helped you overcome challenges and make positive changes in your life.

Discovering Your Strengths Worksheet

1. List the skills and strategies that have helped you the most during your journey through this workbook.

Examples:

- *Skill/Strategy 1: Deep Breathing Exercises*

- *Skill/Strategy 2: Mindfulness Meditation*

- *Skill/Strategy 3: Journaling*

- *Skill/Strategy 4: Problem-Solving Techniques*

2. Identify and write down your strengths and positive qualities that have become evident during this process.

Examples:

- *Strength/Quality 1: Resilience*

- *Strength/Quality 2: Determination*

- *Strength/Quality 3: Empathy*

- *Strength/Quality 4: Creativity*

3. Reflect on how these strengths have helped you overcome challenges and make positive changes in your life. Describe specific instances or situations where your strengths played a crucial role.

Sample Instance 1: Overcoming Exam Stress

- *How did your strengths contribute to overcoming this challenge or achieving a positive change?*

  - *My determination helped me stay focused on studying, and my resilience kept me going even when it got tough. I used deep breathing exercises to manage stress, which improved my concentration.*

- *What did you learn from this experience?*

  - *I learned that I can handle difficult situations with a positive mindset and effective coping strategies.*

Sample Instance 2: Building Better Relationships

- *How did your strengths contribute to overcoming this challenge or achieving a positive change?*

  - *My empathy helped me understand others' perspectives, and my creativity allowed me to come up with thoughtful ways to improve my relationships.*

- *What did you learn from this experience?*

  - *I learned that by being empathetic and creative, I can strengthen my connections with others.*

Sample Instance 3: Solving Personal Problems

- *How did your strengths contribute to overcoming this challenge or achieving a positive change?*

  - *I used problem-solving techniques to address personal issues, and my determination ensured I didn't give up until I found solutions.*

- *What did you learn from this experience?*

○ *I learned that I have the skills and determination to tackle problems effectively and create positive changes in my life.*

Instance:

How did your strengths contribute to overcoming this challenge or achieving a positive change?

What did you learn from this experience?

4. What insights have you gained about yourself during this workbook journey? How have these insights contributed to your personal growth and development?

Sample responses

- *Insight 1: Increased Resilience*

  ○ *Example: I've realized that I'm more resilient than I thought, and this has boosted my confidence in handling challenges.*

- *Insight 2: Enhanced Empathy*

  ○ *Example: My increased empathy has allowed me to connect with others on a deeper level, improving my relationships and communication.*

- *Insight 3: Utilizing Creativity*

  ○ *Example: I've discovered that creativity is a valuable asset for problem-solving and making positive changes in my life.*

Choosing Your Tools

Review the techniques and exercises from earlier chapters that you found most effective and resonated with you. These could include mindfulness practices, problem-solving strategies, or ways to cope with strong emotions.

List these tools and briefly describe how each one works. Consider why they work well for you and how they've made a difference in your life.

Don't worry if you have a long list; you can always narrow it down to the most essential ones in the next step.

Choosing Your Tools Worksheet

1. List the tools and techniques that you have found most effective during your journey through this workbook.

Sample responses

- *Tool/Technique 1: Mindfulness Meditation*

- *Tool/Technique 2: Thought Journaling*

- *Tool/Technique 3: Deep Breathing Exercises*

- *Tool/Technique 4: Problem-Solving Steps*

Tool/Technique 1:
Tool/Technique 2:
Tool/Technique 3:
Tool/Technique 4:

2. Briefly describe how each tool or technique works and why it works well for you. Consider the positive impact it has had on your life.

Sample Responses

Tool/Technique 1: Mindfulness Meditation

- *How it works: Mindfulness meditation involves focusing your attention on the present moment, your breath, or sensations in your body. It helps calm my racing thoughts and reduces stress by grounding me in the here and now.*

- *Why it works well for me: It works well for me because it provides a sense of clarity and relaxation. It's a simple yet powerful way to manage my emotions and stay centered.*

Tool/Technique 2: Thought Journaling

- *How it works: Thought journaling involves writing down my thoughts and feelings, especially when I'm facing a challenge. It helps me identify and challenge negative or unhelpful thoughts.*

- *Why it works well for me: It's effective for me because it allows me to gain perspective on my thoughts. I can see patterns in my thinking and replace unhelpful thoughts with more positive ones.*

Tool/Technique 3: Deep Breathing Exercises

- *How it works: Deep breathing exercises involve taking slow, deep breaths to calm the body's stress response. It helps reduce anxiety and tension.*

- *Why it works well for me: It works well for me because it's a quick and accessible way to manage stress and regain a sense of control when I'm feeling overwhelmed.*

Tool/Technique 4: Problem-Solving Steps

- *How it works: Problem-solving steps provide a structured approach to tackling challenges. It involves identifying the problem, generating solutions, and taking action.*

- *Why it works well for me: It's effective for me because it breaks down complex problems into manageable steps. It empowers me to take action and find solutions, which reduces stress.*

3. Assembling Your Toolbox

Now, it's time to put your chosen tools together into a toolbox that you can access whenever you need them.

You can create a physical toolbox using a real box, container, or even a folder. Alternatively, you can set up a digital toolbox using a note-taking app, a dedicated folder on your computer, or a digital journal.

Customize your toolbox to make it uniquely yours. Add colors, images, stickers, or decorations that resonate with you. This personal touch will make your toolbox feel special and inviting.

Organize your tools within your toolbox, making it easy to locate and use them when facing challenges or striving to manage your emotions.

By completing this section, you'll have a personalized toolbox filled with the strategies and techniques that work best for you. This toolbox will be a valuable resource to support you on your ongoing journey of growth and self-discovery.

Long-term Planning

Vision Board Creation: Instead of setting SMART goals again, let's focus on creating a vision board. A vision board is a visual representation of your dreams and aspirations.

Mapping Your Journey: Visualize the steps it will take to achieve your vision. Create a roadmap that outlines the major milestones and experiences you'll encounter along the way. This map will serve as a flexible guide to keep you on track and motivated.

Connecting with Mentors: Seek out mentors or role models who have achieved similar goals or have valuable life experience. They can provide guidance, advice, and inspiration as you navigate your journey.

Long-term Planning Worksheet

1. Vision Board Creation

- Gather images, words, and symbols that represent your future goals and desires.

- Arrange them on a board or digitally to create a powerful visual representation of your vision.

- Use the space in your journal to describe your vision board and the elements you've included.

Example for Vision Board 1:

- *My vision board includes images of a college campus, a stethoscope (I want to become a doctor), and words like "compassion" and "healthcare." These elements represent my dream of pursuing a career in medicine and making a difference in people's lives.*

Example for Vision Board 2:

- *I have created a digital vision board using a collage app. It features images that symbolize my dream of becoming a successful author. There are pictures of books, a laptop, and a serene writing space. I've also included motivational quotes about writing and achieving goals.*

2. Mapping Your Journey

- Visualize the steps it will take to achieve your vision.

- Create a roadmap that outlines the major milestones and experiences you'll encounter along the way.

- Use the space in your journal to describe your roadmap and the key milestones you've identified.

Example for Mapping Your Journey 1:

- *Alright, so here's the plan: first up, acing high school and snagging that diploma. Then, it's off to a killer internship in coding to beef up my tech skills. After that, I'm hitting up college for computer science and diving deep into the world of app development. Finally, I'll launch my own startup and revolutionize the digital world with my groundbreaking apps!*

Example for Mapping Your Journey 2:

- *Here's my roadmap for chasing my dreams in the music biz: Step one, master those guitar chords and start jamming with friends. Next, it's all about hitting the local scene, playing gigs, and building a fanbase. Then, I'll take my skills to the next level with music school and dive into songwriting and production. Finally, I'll be headlining major festivals and dropping albums that'll rock the charts!*

3. Connecting with Mentors

- Identify potential mentors or role models who have achieved similar goals or have valuable life experience.

- Use the space in your journal to list the names and contact information of potential mentors you'd like to connect with.

Example for Connecting with Mentors:

- *Mentor 1:*

  - *Name: Dr. Emily Carter*

  - *Contact: emily.carter@email.com*

  - *Reason for Connection: Dr. Carter is a successful pediatrician, which aligns with my career aspirations. I'd like to learn from her experiences and seek guidance on my journey to becoming a doctor.*

- *Mentor 2:*

  - *Name: Sarah Johnson*

  - *Contact: sarah.johnson@author.com*

  - *Reason for Connection: Sarah is a published author who has achieved the kind of success I aspire to in my writing career. I hope to connect with her to gain insights into the world of publishing.*

> it would be cool to see a non-white example for mentors!

Reflection and Growth

Journaling for Self-Reflection: Keep a journal to document your thoughts, feelings, and experiences as you continue your journey. Use it as a tool to gain insight into your progress and challenges.

Adapting Your Strategies: Life is always changing, and so are your needs. Regularly review and adapt the strategies in your toolbox to meet new challenges and opportunities that come your way.

Celebrating Your Success: Don't forget to celebrate your achievements, no matter how small they may seem. Celebrations help boost your motivation and self-esteem.

Reflection and Growth Worksheet

1. Journaling for Self-Reflection

- Set aside time regularly to journal your thoughts, feelings, and experiences.

- Use your journal as a tool to gain insight into your progress and challenges.

- Reflect on your personal growth journey and how the strategies you've learned have made a difference.

Example for Journaling for Self-Reflection 1

- *I've started a journal to document my experiences as I pursue my dream of becoming a doctor. I write about my daily activities, challenges, and moments of inspiration. I also use it to reflect on my personal growth and the impact of the strategies I've learned from this workbook.*

Example for Journaling for Self-Reflection 2

- *My journal has become a valuable companion on my journey. It helps me process my emotions, track my progress, and stay motivated. I've noticed that writing down my thoughts allows me to gain clarity and discover new insights.*

2. Adapting Your Strategies

- Life is constantly changing, and so are your needs.

- Regularly review the strategies in your toolbox and assess their effectiveness.

- Be open to adapting and adding new techniques to meet new challenges and opportunities.

Example for Adapting Your Strategies

- *As I navigate through the ups and downs of high school, I've noticed that my go-to study methods aren't hitting the mark like they used to. Instead of sticking to the same old routine, I'm mixing things up and trying out different study techniques to keep things fresh and effective.*

Strategy Adaptation

- *Switching up my study game has been crucial for keeping me on track. It keeps me motivated and eager to find what works best for me. I've come to realize that being willing to try new approaches helps me overcome any academic hurdles and keeps my learning journey exciting and rewarding.*

3. Celebrating Your Success

- Take time to acknowledge and celebrate your achievements, no matter how small they may seem.

- Celebrations boost your motivation, self-esteem, and overall sense of accomplishment.

- Use the space in your journal to list recent achievements you'd like to celebrate.

Example for Celebrating Your Success

- *Achievement 1: Finally aced that tough math exam after weeks of grinding and late-night study sessions.*

- *Achievement 2: Scored the lead role in the school play after months of auditions and rehearsals.*

- *Achievement 3: Crushed it in the big game, scoring the winning goal and leading our team to victory.*

- *Celebrations: To celebrate these wins, I gathered my squad for a movie marathon and pizza party. It was the perfect way to unwind, bond with friends, and toast to our hard-earned victories.*

Remember, this is your personal journey, and there's no right or wrong way to go about it. You have the power to shape your future and create a fulfilling life aligned with your values and aspirations. Keep using your toolbox, stay connected to your goals, and continue to grow as the amazing person you are!

10

Navigating Tough Terrain

As we near the end of our journey, we're diving into a special bonus chapter. This section is all about tackling the tricky situations, the moments that make you scratch your head, and the times when things might not be going as planned. It's like having a compass for the challenges that can pop up unexpectedly on your path to thriving.

In this bonus chapter, we'll be exploring how to troubleshoot when it feels like nothing's working, how to handle encounters with not-so-nice people, and even a section to keep things real and remind you that, well, you're not the center of the universe. So buckle up, because we're about to dive into some real-talk strategies and insights that will empower you to navigate life's rough patches with confidence and grace.

Section 1: When Things Seem Tough: What to Do When Nothing Works

We get it – life can throw some serious curveballs, and there might be moments when it feels like none of the tools you've learned so far are doing the trick. Guess what? That's totally okay. In this section, we're diving into what to do when it seems like nothing's going your way. Let's explore some real-talk strategies for those tough times:

It's Okay to Let It Out

First things first, let's give you permission to feel whatever you're feeling. Sometimes, a good ol' scream into a pillow or a heartfelt cry can be the ultimate release. Emotions are like waves, and it's totally fine to ride them.

Reaching Out to Adults

Guess what? Adults were teenagers once, too. They've faced their fair share of challenges and might have some wisdom to share. Don't be afraid to lean on them when things feel overwhelming. Sometimes, their life experiences can offer a fresh perspective.

Finding Additional Resources

You know what's cool? There's a world of information out there waiting for you. Books, articles, podcasts – you name it. Exploring these resources can provide you with new insights and tools to deal with the challenges that come your way.

It's Okay to Not Have All the Answers

You're not expected to be a superhero 24/7. There will be times when things just don't make sense, and that's okay. It's all part of this wild journey called life.

Remember, even when it seems like everything's upside down, you're not alone. Lean on those around you, give yourself permission to feel, and remember that tough times don't last forever. You've got this!

Section 2: Dealing with Mean People: Strategies for Handling Difficult Situations

Recognizing Different Types of Negativity

Life isn't all unicorns and rainbows, and there will be moments when you encounter negativity from others. This part is about getting real – not everyone you meet will radiate positivity. Some people might throw shade, criticize, or bring down the vibe. It's key to spot these types of negativity, so you're ready to respond with your head held high. By knowing the different flavors of negativity, you'll be the master of your reactions.

Scenario

Imagine you're at a school event, and someone makes a snarky comment about your outfit. This is the "jealousy" category. Your clever response could be a playful wink and saying, "Oh, thanks! I guess my style is too much of a vibe for some." With this comeback, you don't let their negativity dim your sparkle, and you keep the situation light.

Clever Comebacks:

- "Thanks for your opinion, but I'm my own fashion icon."

- "You must really care about my choices to comment on them."

- "I guess we have different taste, and that's cool!"

- "Your comments say more about you than they do about me."

- "Oh, I love how confident you are sharing your opinions!"

- "My style's a bit unconventional – not everyone gets it."

- "I'm not here to fit in; I'm here to stand out!"

- "I think my outfit just broke the fashion meter."

- "I'm rocking my unique style – care to join the trend?"

- "My clothes reflect my personality; what about yours?"

Responding with Assertiveness and Confidence: *remove*

Dealing with negativity is like facing a dragon – you gotta stand your ground. This section is all about rocking your confidence and responding like the rock star you are. Remember, your feelings matter, and you don't have to take any nonsense. Being assertive is your secret weapon to shut down negativity while keeping your cool.

Scenario

Picture this: you're sharing your idea in a group discussion, and someone interrupts you with a dismissive tone. You calmly pause and say, "I wasn't done speaking, and my idea has some serious potential." Your assertive response puts them in their place while showcasing your confidence and determination.

Assertive Comebacks:

- "Hold on, I'd like to finish my point."

- "I appreciate your input, but let's hear everyone out."

- "I'm not done sharing my idea – it's worth listening to."

- "Interrupting doesn't help us have a productive discussion."

- "Let's give each person a chance to speak, one at a time."

- "I'll be happy to hear your thoughts once I've finished."

- "My idea deserves the same respect as everyone else's."

- "Interrupting is distracting – let's keep it focused."

- "We're all here to contribute; let's make sure everyone can."

- "Thanks for your enthusiasm, but let's keep things organized."

Setting Boundaries with Toxic Individuals

Fact check: not everyone will be your #1 fan. Some people might bring toxic vibes into your orbit. This section is about knowing when someone's negativity is toxic and setting boundaries like a pro. It's like putting up a "No Toxicity Allowed" sign in your emotional space. By defining your limits, you create a safe zone for positivity.

Scenario

Imagine you have a friend who always finds something negative to say about your accomplishments. This level of negativity is a toxic alert. You could say, "I'm excited about my achievements, and I expect my friends to be supportive." With this boundary-setting line, you make it clear that their toxicity won't be tolerated in your circle.

Boundary-Setting Comebacks:

- "I'm all about positive vibes – let's keep it that way."

- "Negative comments aren't really my thing; let's focus on uplifting conversations."

- "I'm here to support and be supported – that's how we roll."

- "I'm on a positivity mission – care to join?"

- "Negative energy isn't allowed in my space."

- "If you can't be supportive, let's just stick to neutral topics."

- "I'm all ears for encouragement, not criticism."

- "My circle is for those who lift each other up."

- "I'm putting my mental well-being first – negativity won't fit."

- "My vibes are reserved for positivity; wanna be part of that?"

Keeping Your Cool and Rising Above

When mean comments come your way, it's time to show your emotional ninja skills. This part is all about keeping your cool while mean people do their thing. Remember, their negativity isn't your problem – it's theirs. Rising above mean remarks is like taking the high road while they're stuck in the negativity lane.

Scenario

Let's say someone tries to put you down by saying, "You're never going to make it in that field." Instead of getting defensive, you smile and reply, "I appreciate your opinion, but I believe in my path." By keeping your cool and responding with grace, you show that their negativity can't touch your confidence.

Rising Above Comebacks:

- "I'm focused on my journey – negativity can't slow me down."

- "I'm confident in my choices – thanks for your input though!"

- "My journey is mine to own, and I'm proud of it."

- "I'm too busy working on my goals to engage in negativity."

- "I'm on a positivity streak – no room for negativity here."

- "Your comments won't change my course – I'm determined."

- "I respect your thoughts, but I'm staying true to myself."

- "I'm soaring above negativity – care to join the flight?"

- "It's interesting how opinions can differ so much."

No matter how much negativity floats around, you've got the tools to handle it like a champ. Recognize the vibes, respond with clever comebacks, set boundaries like a boss, and rise above the noise. Remember, you're the captain of your ship, and you decide which waves to ride.

Section 3: Keeping It Real: Gaining Perspective and Balance

Understanding the "Center of the Universe" Mindset

Picture yourself at the center of a swirling galaxy of thoughts and attention. Welcome to the teenage mindset, where it's like you're the sun and everything else revolves around you. It's not just you – it's a phase that comes with this journey of self-discovery. This section is all about taking a cosmic perspective on why you might feel like the universe is fixated on your every move.

Getting Real

Imagine a stage with you as the lead actor. You're under the spotlight, and every move, every outfit choice, every word you say feels magnified. Here's the secret: every other teen is under their spotlight too. This is the time when you're crafting your identity and figuring out where you belong, so naturally, it feels like you're in the center. But guess what? Everyone else is starring in their own show too.

Recognizing Everyone's Role in the Bigger Picture

Now, let's zoom out from the cosmic stage and gaze at the vast expanse of humanity. Just like stars in the night sky, everyone has their own brilliance. This section is about realizing that while you're shining, so is everyone else. It's like looking up and realizing you're part of a dazzling constellation.

Gaining Perspective

Remember that time you tripped in the hallway and felt like the world was watching? Chances are, they were too caught up in their own stories to notice. People are wrapped up in their lives, just like you are. So, that spotlight? It's a shared experience. Your slip-up might be a momentary thought for someone else, just like theirs is for you.

Fostering Empathy and Understanding

Empathy is your telescope to understanding others. The "center of the universe" mindset isn't about being self-centered; it's part of growing up. This section is like putting on empathy glasses that let you see the challenges and triumphs of others. It's realizing that every star has its own path through the sky.

Empathy Exercise

Next time you're feeling the heat of the spotlight, think about that person across the room who might be feeling the same. Extend a hand of kindness, share a smile – these simple actions bridge the gap between your spotlight and theirs.

Finding Balance Between Self-Importance and Humility

Imagine you're a star in a constellation – unique, radiant, but part of a bigger picture. This section is all about finding equilibrium between being the protagonist of your story and realizing that you're an extra in many others. It's the cosmic dance of identity and humility.

Balancing Act

Sure, you're the main character in your narrative, but you're also a co-star in everyone else's. Every person has dreams, challenges, and stories to tell. While you're shining your brightest, remember that the universe is filled with countless stories, each as significant as yours.

In a Cosmic Shell

Teenhood is like standing in the center of your universe, but it's a universe full of other stars with their own orbits. You're the architect of your identity, but so is everyone else. The next time a minor hiccup threatens to eclipse your brilliance, remind yourself that the cosmic ballet continues, and you're an integral part of it. So, keep shining, keep exploring, and keep it real!

Embracing a Thriving Lifestyle: Your Foundation for Success

You've journeyed through the pages of this book and unlocked a treasure trove of strategies to navigate life's twists and turns. As you stand at the final crossroads of this adventure, let's dive into a vital truth: the tools you've acquired are powerful, but they are only part of the equation.

Imagine your newfound strategies as the sails of a ship, guiding you through stormy seas. Yet, even the sturdiest vessel requires a solid foundation to weather the elements. That foundation, dear adventurers, is built upon the core healthy lifestyle habits that sustain your mental and emotional well-being.

These habits are the bedrock of your journey towards a thriving life. They fuel the effectiveness of the tools you've gathered, ensuring they work in harmony with your body and mind. Without this foundation, even the mightiest strategies may fall short of their potential.

So, let's take a moment to revisit the pillars of a healthy lifestyle:

1. **Quality Sleep:** Your brain craves rest like a desert craves rain. Aim for a consistent 8 hours of sleep each night, and stick to a regular sleep schedule. Adequate sleep revitalizes your mind, enhances memory, and promotes emotional resilience.

2. **Good Nutrition:** Think of your body as a high-performance vehicle – it needs the right fuel. Nutrient-rich foods, including fruits, vegetables, whole grains, and lean proteins, provide the sustenance your body and brain require to function optimally.

3. **Physical Activity:** The joy of movement isn't just a saying – it's backed by science. Engage in regular physical activity that you enjoy. Exercise releases endorphins, which are your brain's natural mood enhancers. It improves focus, reduces stress, and boosts overall well-being.

4. **Minimal Screen Time:** Your devices are portals to fascinating worlds, but too much screen time can cast shadows on your mental health. Set boundaries on your screen use to prevent it from interfering with your sleep, productivity, and social interactions.

As you reflect on your journey and the tools you've acquired, remember that these core lifestyle habits are the key to unlocking their full potential. If you find yourself facing challenges or questioning the effectiveness of the strategies, pause and reflect. Are you consistently nurturing these healthy habits? Are they the solid foundation upon which you're building your thriving life?

Just as a garden requires sunlight, water, and care to flourish, your journey to mental and emotional well-being thrives on these core habits. They nourish your mind, energize your body, and provide the optimal conditions for your strategies to take root and blossom.

So, let this be your final reminder, fellow adventurers: as you venture forth into the world armed with your newfound knowledge, ensure that you're nurturing the foundation of a healthy lifestyle. Quality sleep, good nutrition, physical activity, and minimal screen time are the threads that weave your success story.

May your sails catch the winds of resilience, and may your foundation remain unwavering as you navigate the seas of life. Your journey doesn't end here – it continues with each step you take towards embracing a thriving lifestyle. Keep the tools close, nurture your foundation, and remember that you hold the power to conquer challenges and thrive, no matter what storms may come. Onward, intrepid souls, to a life of flourishing!

Appendix A

Here is a list of 100 emotions separated into 4 categories: sad or low-energy emotions, anxious or high-energy emotions, intense or aggressive emotions, and calm or neutral emotions.

Sad/Low:

Sad, Depressed, Lonely, Mournful, Grief-stricken, Heartbroken, Tearful, Desolate, Dismal, Downhearted, Woeful, Forlorn, Blue, Sorrowful, Regretful, Down in the dumps, Melancholic, Despondent, Tearful, Lonesome, Forlorn, Blue, Sorrowful.

Anxious/High-energy:

Anxious, Nervous, Apprehensive, Worried, Tense, Uneasy, Restless, Panicked, Scared, Timid, Shy, Self-conscious, Embarrassed, Awkward, Vulnerable, Inferior, Inadequate, Worthless, Insecure, Uncertain, Confused, Perplexed, Baffled, Lost, Disoriented, Bewildered, Overwhelmed, Stressed, Hysterical, Apprehensive.

Intense/Aggressive:

Angry, Furious, Enraged, Resentful, Irritated, Frustrated, Mad, Outraged, Incensed, Wrathful, Hostile, Raging, Indignant, Cross, Annoyed, Aggravated, Explosive, Outburst, Furious, Irate, Wrathful.

Calm/Neutral:

Happy, Excited, Content, Joyful, Ecstatic, Delighted, Overjoyed, Euphoric, Optimistic, Cheerful, Grateful, Thankful, Pleased, Comfortable, Fulfilled, Serene, Relieved, Calm, Peaceful, Satisfied, Radiant, Appreciative, Joyous, Energetic, Lively, Playful

APPENDIX B

Here is a list of 25 values:

Authenticity, Kindness, Respect, Empathy, Gratitude, Acceptance, Friendship, Loyalty, Individuality, Creativity, Positivity, Self-expression, Inclusivity, Confidence, Ambition, Resilience, Freedom, Adventure, Fun, Sustainability, Social justice, Equality, Independence, Innovation, Empowerment.

APPENDIX C

This section presents a list of 30 common cognitive distortions along with relatable situations. It aims to help teenagers recognize and challenge these distorted thinking patterns, promoting healthier and more realistic thought processes for better mental health and well-being.

School Situations

1. Situation: You received a lower grade than you expected on a test.

- **Automatic Thought:** "I'm a total failure."

- **Cognitive Distortion:** All-or-Nothing Thinking (Black and White Thinking)

- **Feelings:** Disappointment, Frustration

- **Reframed Thought:** "While I didn't do as well as I hoped, it's just one test, and it doesn't define my abilities. I can learn from my mistakes and aim for improvement next time."

- **More Helpful Alternative:** Acknowledging areas for growth and setting goals for improvement can lead to better outcomes in the future.

- **Behavior Change:** Create a study plan for the next test, focusing on areas where you can improve.

2. Situation: You have a big project due tomorrow.

- **Automatic Thought:** "I can't handle this; it's too much pressure."

- **Cognitive Distortion:** Catastrophizing (Magnification and Minimization)

- **Feelings:** Overwhelmed, Stress

- **Reframed Thought:** "While this is a challenging task, I can break it down into smaller steps and manage my time effectively. It's a chance to demonstrate my skills and learning."

- **More Helpful Alternative:** Breaking tasks into manageable parts and planning ahead can reduce stress and lead to better performance.

- **Behavior Change:** Create a detailed task list and allocate time to complete each part of the project.

3. Situation: You were asked to answer a question in class, and you couldn't.

- **Automatic Thought:** "Everyone thinks I'm stupid."

- **Cognitive Distortion:** Mind Reading

- **Feelings:** Embarrassment, Insecurity

- **Reframed Thought:** "It's okay not to know the answer every time. No one can read minds, and I can learn from this experience by asking questions to improve my understanding."

- **More Helpful Alternative:** Accepting that everyone makes mistakes and seeking help or clarification when needed can boost confidence.

- **Behavior Change:** Make an effort to participate more actively in class discussions and ask questions when you're unsure.

4. Situation: Your friends are all in the same class except you.

- **Automatic Thought:** "I'm always left out."

- **Cognitive Distortion:** Overgeneralization

- **Feelings:** Left Out, Isolation

- **Reframed Thought:** "This might be an opportunity to meet new people and have different experiences. Just because we're not in the same class doesn't mean I'm always left out."

- **More Helpful Alternative:** Embracing new opportunities and being open to making new friends can lead to enriching experiences.

- **Behavior Change:** Seek out social activities or clubs where you can meet new people who share your interests.

5. Situation: You have to give a presentation in front of the class.

- **Automatic Thought:** "I'm going to mess up and look like a fool."

- **Cognitive Distortion:** Fortune Telling (Jumping to Conclusions)

- **Feelings:** Anxiety, Fear

- **Reframed Thought:** "While I may feel nervous, I can prepare and practice to the best of my ability. Mistakes are a part of learning and growing, and they don't define my worth."

- **More Helpful Alternative:** Accepting that everyone makes mistakes and viewing challenges as opportunities for growth can reduce anxiety.

- **Behavior Change:** Practice your presentation multiple times and consider seeking feedback from peers or instructors.

6. Situation: Your teacher didn't praise your work like they did for others.

- **Automatic Thought:** "I'm not good enough."

- **Cognitive Distortion:** Discounting the Positive

- **Feelings**: Inadequacy, Sadness

- **Reframed Thought:** "Recognition is nice, but I'll focus on doing my best for personal satisfaction and improvement. One person's opinion doesn't define my abilities."

- **More Helpful Alternative:** Finding intrinsic motivation and deriving satisfaction from personal growth can lead to more sustainable efforts.

- **Behavior Change:** Continue to invest effort and time in your studies for your own growth and learning, rather than seeking external validation.

7. Situation: You didn't get invited to a study group.

- **Automatic Thought:** "Nobody likes me."

- **Cognitive Distortion:** Magnification and Minimization (Catastrophizing)

- **Feelings**: Rejection, Loneliness

- **Reframed Thought:** "Maybe they already had a full group or preferred a different study approach. I can find other study options and focus on my own learning."

- **More Helpful Alternative:** Seeking alternative study methods or groups and not taking rejection personally can lead to more productive learning experiences.

- **Behavior Change:** Explore other study resources or consider forming a study group with classmates who have similar goals.

8. Situation: You have a disagreement with a friend about a school project.

- **Automatic Thought:** "They must hate me now."

- **Cognitive Distortion:** Emotional Reasoning

- **Feelings**: Anger, Frustration

- **Reframed Thought:** "Disagreements happen, and it doesn't mean our friendship is in jeopardy. We can work together to find a solution and learn from this experience."

- **More Helpful Alternative:** Approaching conflicts with open communication and problem-solving can strengthen friendships.

- **Behavior Change:** Reach out to your friend to discuss the disagreement calmly and find a mutually acceptable resolution.

9. Situation: You made a spelling mistake in your essay.

- **Automatic Thought:** "I'm so stupid."

- **Cognitive Distortion:** Labeling and Mislabeling

- **Feelings:** Embarrassment, Regret

- **Reframed Thought:** "Mistakes are common, and I can proofread more carefully next time. Making a spelling error doesn't define my intelligence or worth."

- **More Helpful Alternative:** Embracing imperfections and using them as opportunities for improvement can lead to personal growth.

- **Behavior Change:** Develop a thorough proofreading process for future writing assignments to catch and correct errors.

10. Situation: You're anxious about upcoming final exams.

- **Automatic Thought:** "I'm going to fail and ruin my future."

- **Cognitive Distortion:** Catastrophizing

- **Feelings:** Anxiety, Stress

- **Reframed Thought:** "Feeling nervous is natural, and I can use that energy to focus on effective studying and preparation. One exam doesn't determine my entire future."

- **More Helpful Alternative:** Accepting and managing exam-related stress through practical study strategies and self-care can lead to better performance.

- **Behavior Change:** Create a structured study plan, practice relaxation techniques, and ensure adequate rest to optimize exam preparation and reduce anxiety.

Friendship Situations

1. Situation: Your friend didn't reply to your message for hours.

- **Automatic Thought:** "They're probably mad at me."

- **Cognitive Distortion:** Personalization

- **Feelings:** Anxiety, Insecurity

- **Reframed Thought:** "They might be busy or didn't see my message yet. It doesn't necessarily mean they're mad at me."

- **More Helpful Alternative:** Giving people the benefit of the doubt and avoiding assumptions can maintain healthier relationships.

- **Behavior Change:** Reach out to your friend with a friendly message or wait patiently for their response without jumping to conclusions.

2. Situation: You saw your friends hanging out without inviting you.

- **Automatic Thought:** "I'm not important to them."

- **Cognitive Distortion:** Mind Reading

- **Feelings**: Rejection, Hurt

- **Reframed Thought:** "They might have made plans without considering me this time. It doesn't mean I'm not important overall."

- **More Helpful Alternative:** Recognizing that friends have various social interactions and not taking it personally can reduce negative emotions.

- **Behavior Change:** Plan your own social activities or reach out to your friends to arrange a get-together, fostering inclusivity.

3. Situation: Your friend posted pictures from a fun outing, and you weren't invited.

- **Automatic Thought:** "I must be boring or annoying."

- **Cognitive Distortion:** Overgeneralization

- **Feelings:** Inadequacy, Sadness

- **Reframed Thought:** "People have different social circles and interests. It doesn't reflect my worth as a person."

- **More Helpful Alternative:** Embracing individuality and understanding that not every social event includes everyone can lead to greater self-acceptance.

- **Behavior Change:** Focus on your own interests and passions, seeking opportunities to connect with people who share your values and hobbies.

4. Situation: Your friend made a joke about your appearance.

- **Automatic Thought:** "They think I look ugly."

- **Cognitive Distortion:** Mind Reading

- **Feelings:** Insecurity, Embarrassment

- **Reframed Thought:** "My friend's comment may have been in jest or without ill intentions. It doesn't define my overall attractiveness."

- **More Helpful Alternative:** Communicating openly with friends about boundaries and feelings can maintain healthy friendships.

- **Behavior Change:** If you feel uncomfortable with such comments, calmly express your boundaries and let your friend know how their comments affect you.

5. Situation: You had a disagreement with your best friend.

- **Automatic Thought:** "Our friendship is over."

- **Cognitive Distortion:** Catastrophizing

- **Feelings:** Fear, Sadness

- **Reframed Thought:** "Disagreements are part of any relationship. Our friendship can become stronger if we communicate and resolve conflicts together."

- **More Helpful Alternative:** Viewing conflicts as opportunities for growth and resolution can lead to stronger friendships.

- **Behavior Change:** Initiate a conversation with your friend to address the disagreement and work together to find a resolution that benefits both parties.

6. Situation: You overheard your friends talking and laughing without you.

- **Automatic Thought:** "They're probably making fun of me."

- **Cognitive Distortion:** Mind Reading

- **Feelings:** Hurt, Paranoia

- **Reframed Thought:** "It's natural for friends to enjoy each other's company. It doesn't mean they're talking negatively about me."

- **More Helpful Alternative:** Trusting in the bonds of friendship and avoiding unnecessary assumptions can reduce anxiety.

- **Behavior Change:** Approach your friends and join the conversation with a positive and open attitude, avoiding overthinking.

7. Situation: Your friends have different plans, and you weren't invited.

- **Automatic Thought:** "I'm not good enough for them."

- **Cognitive Distortion**: Overgeneralization

- **Feelings:** Rejection, Insecurity

- **Reframed Thought:** "People have various interests and commitments. It doesn't diminish my value as a friend."

- **More Helpful Alternative:** Recognizing that friendships can coexist with individuality and different plans can foster self-confidence.

- **Behavior Change:** Create opportunities for group activities or engage in individual hobbies and interests that boost your self-esteem and self-worth.

8. Situation: A friend canceled plans with you.

- **Automatic Thought:** "They don't really like spending time with me."

- **Cognitive Distortion:** Personalization

- **Feelings:** Disappointment, Insecurity

- **Reframed Thought:** "Life can be unpredictable, and plans change. It doesn't mean my friend doesn't value our time together."

- **More Helpful Alternative:** Understanding that cancellations can occur for various reasons and not taking it as a personal rejection can preserve relationships.

- **Behavior Change:** Express your understanding and willingness to reschedule when your friend is available, maintaining a positive and flexible attitude.

9. Situation: You saw a friend liking and commenting on other people's social media posts but not yours.

- **Automatic Thought:** "They're avoiding me."

- **Cognitive Distortion:** Mind Reading

- **Feelings:** Rejection, Insecurity

- **Reframed Thought:** "Social media interactions don't always reflect real-life relationships. There could be various reasons for this, and it doesn't mean my friend is avoiding me."

- **More Helpful Alternative:** Not overanalyzing online interactions and valuing in-person connections can improve well-being.

- **Behavior Change:** Focus on building genuine, offline connections with your friend and avoid comparing social media activities.

10. Situation: You got into an argument with a friend over something trivial.

- **Automatic Thought:** "Our friendship is falling apart."

- **Cognitive Distortion:** Catastrophizing

- **Feelings:** Fear, Sadness

- **Reframed Thought:** "Arguments can happen in any relationship, and they don't necessarily indicate the end of our friendship. We can work through this."

- **More Helpful Alternative:** Viewing conflicts as opportunities for growth and resolution can lead to stronger friendships.

- **Behavior Change:** Initiate a conversation with your friend to address the disagreement and work together to find a resolution that benefits both parties.

Family Situations

1. Situation: Your parents had an argument.

- **Automatic Thought:** "It's my fault; they're fighting because of me."

- **Cognitive Distortion:** Personalization

- **Feelings:** Guilt, Anxiety

- **Reframed Thought:** "Arguments can happen between adults for various reasons, and it's not my responsibility. I can communicate my feelings if I'm affected."

- **More Helpful Alternative:** Recognizing that adults have their own dynamics and setting boundaries in communication can reduce unnecessary guilt.

- **Behavior Change:** Express your feelings and concerns calmly to your parents when appropriate, but avoid blaming yourself for their conflicts.

2. Situation: Your parents set strict rules, and you feel trapped.

- **Automatic Thought:** "They don't trust me at all."

- **Cognitive Distortion:** Catastrophizing

- **Feelings:** Frustration, Rebellion

- **Reframed Thought:** "My parents have rules to keep me safe and help me learn responsibility. It doesn't mean they don't trust me; it's about guidance."

- **More Helpful Alternative:** Viewing rules as a form of support and learning can lead to a more constructive perspective.

- **Behavior Change:** Engage in a respectful conversation with your parents to better understand their reasons behind the rules and express your desire for more responsibility while proving your reliability.

3. Situation: Your sibling borrowed your things without asking.

- **Automatic Thought:** "They're so disrespectful."

- **Cognitive Distortion:** Labeling and Mislabeling

- **Feelings:** Anger, Resentment

- **Reframed Thought:** "My sibling may not have realized it bothered me, and we can talk about boundaries. It doesn't mean they're disrespectful as a whole."

- **More Helpful Alternative:** Open communication and setting boundaries can improve sibling relationships.

- **Behavior Change:** Have a calm conversation with your sibling about respecting personal belongings and establish clear boundaries for sharing items.

4. Situation: Your parents criticize your choices.

- **Automatic Thought:** "They don't believe in me."

- **Cognitive Distortion:** Mind Reading

- **Feelings:** Insecurity, Hurt

- **Reframed Thought:** "My parents' criticism may come from concern and wanting the best for me. It doesn't mean they don't believe in my abilities."

- **More Helpful Alternative:** Engaging in constructive discussions with parents about choices and goals can lead to better understanding.

- **Behavior Change:** Listen to your parents' concerns and explain your reasoning and plans when discussing important choices, aiming for a more open and understanding conversation.

5. Situation: Your parents forgot an important event in your life.

- **Automatic Thought:** "They don't care about me."

- **Cognitive Distortion:** Overgeneralization

- **Feelings:** Disappointment, Neglect

- **Reframed Thought:** "People can forget things, and it doesn't diminish their love and care for me overall. I can communicate my feelings."

- **More Helpful Alternative:** Openly discussing feelings and needs with parents can strengthen the parent-child relationship.

- **Behavior Change:** Politely remind your parents about the event and express how important it is to you, fostering better communication and understanding.

6. Situation: Your parents compared you to a sibling.

- **Automatic Thought:** "They like them better."

- **Cognitive Distortion:** Overgeneralization

- **Feelings:** Jealousy, Insecurity

- **Reframed Thought:** "Parents may have different ways of showing support and love. It doesn't mean they like one of us more."

- **More Helpful Alternative:** Acknowledging individuality and discussing feelings with parents can foster understanding.

- **Behavior Change:** Have an open and honest conversation with your parents about how comparisons make you feel, and ask for their support in recognizing your individual strengths.

7. Situation: Your parents are strict about curfew.

- **Automatic Thought:** "They're just trying to control me."

- **Cognitive Distortion:** Mind Reading

- **Feelings:** Frustration, Rebellion

- **Reframed Thought:** "Curfew rules are about safety and responsibility. It doesn't mean they're controlling me; it's about mutual respect."

- **More Helpful Alternative:** Understanding rules in the context of safety and communication can lead to a more positive perspective.

- **Behavior Change:** Discuss curfew expectations with your parents, emphasizing your commitment to safety, and propose a compromise that respects both their concerns and your growing independence.

8. Situation: You had an argument with your parents about your future plans.

- **Automatic Thought:** "They don't understand me at all."

- **Cognitive Distortion:** Emotional Reasoning

- **Feelings:** Frustration, Misunderstood

- **Reframed Thought:** "We have different perspectives, and that's okay. It doesn't mean they don't care; it's a chance for communication and compromise."

- **More Helpful Alternative:** Engaging in open discussions and seeking compromises can improve understanding.

- **Behavior Change:** Initiate a calm and respectful conversation with your parents, actively listening to their concerns, and expressing your viewpoint with empathy to find common ground.

9. Situation: Your parents didn't approve of a friend.

- **Automatic Thought:** "They're trying to ruin my social life."

- **Cognitive Distortion:** Catastrophizing

- **Feelings:** Anger, Defiance

- **Reframed Thought:** "My parents may have concerns for my well-being. It doesn't mean they want to ruin my social life; it's about safety and guidance."

- **More Helpful Alternative:** Discussing concerns with parents and finding a balance between friendships and family can lead to a more harmonious approach.

- **Behavior Change:** Have an open conversation with your parents about your friend, addressing their concerns while expressing your understanding of their worries and your commitment to responsible choices.

10. Situation: Your family has a tradition you don't enjoy.

- **Automatic Thought:** "They never listen to what I want."

- **Cognitive Distortion:** Personalization

- **Feelings:** Frustration, Resentment

- **Reframed Thought:** "My family may not be aware of my feelings about this tradition. It's an opportunity to communicate my preferences and find compromises."

- **More Helpful Alternative:** Openly sharing feelings and suggestions with family members can lead to a more enjoyable family experience.

- **Behavior Change:** Approach your family with your concerns and alternative ideas for family traditions, fostering a more inclusive and enjoyable atmosphere for everyone.